ABOUT THE COVER

The photo (painting) on the front cover captures the essence of the Nimrods en route to yet another life-or-death combat mission in the Vietnam War. This incredibly beautiful and authentic A-26 Counter Invader painting resulted from the collaborative efforts of internationally known aviation artist Harley Copic and A-26 armorer and aviation art enthusiast Paul Tobey. All Nimrods appreciate this beautiful painting. The painting shows a pilot and navigator/co-pilot heading east after take-off from Nakhon Phanom Royal Thai Air Force Base in Thailand. It is dusk and the sun is setting in the west. The darkening storm clouds foreshadow a rendezvous with destiny. This copyrighted photo of the painting is reprinted with the permission of Harley Copic, the artist, and Paul Tobey, the owner of the painting.

THE NIMRODS

by

Roger D. Graham, Colonel, USAF-Retired

authorHOUSE®

AuthorHouse™
1663 Liberty Drive, Suite 200
Bloomington, IN 47403
www.authorhouse.com
Phone: 1-800-839-8640

First published by AuthorHouse 9/17/2007

ISBN: 978-1-4343-1727-8 (sc)
ISBN: 978-1-4343-2463-4 (hc)

Printed in the United States of America
Bloomington, Indiana

This book is printed on acid-free paper.

THE NIMRODS

A-26 NIMRODS AND THE SECRET WAR IN LAOS...
TIMELESS AMERICAN COURAGE IN COMBAT

LESSONS LEARNED FOR THE WARS IN IRAQ AND
AFGHANISTAN, AND THE WAR ON TERROR

WRITTEN BY ROGER D. GRAHAM
COLONEL, USAF-RETIRED

TABLE OF CONTENTS

DEDICATION

To my father, Frank Joseph Graham, Private, U.S. Army, American soldier, Killed in Action, Battle of the Bulge, Belgium, two miles east of Bastogne, January 5, 1945.

To my mother, Dorothy Graham Montgomery, who suffered the loss of my father but found the strength to raise her three small children: Shirley, Daniel and Roger.

To my wife Dianne, and to our children, Kimberly, Kristi (and husband Bill) and Ryan, and to our grandchildren, Colette, Averi and Chase, and to our extended family.

To the Nimrods, and to all American combat veterans and members of their families who bear the burden and pay the price for Freedom in the United States of America.

CHAPTER 1: WHO WERE THE NIMRODS?

As I reflect back on flying combat missions in the Vietnam War, I believe that I had the privilege of being a member of one of the most unique combat units in American military history. This story is permanently engrained in my mind. I can close my eyes on any given day or night and think back to what it was like to fly nighttime A-26 Invader dive-bombing missions in the Vietnam War in 1967-68. We primarily flew bombing missions in Steel Tiger and Barrel Roll in Laos, but we also flew bombing missions into North Vietnam and South Vietnam. We were the Nimrods...the 609th Air Commando Squadron based at Nakhon Phanom Royal Thai Air Force Base (RTAFB), Thailand. I was most fortunate to have survived 182 of those combat missions. Our story has not been told until now. I would like to share it with you.

If I close my eyes, I immediately see darkness and the sight of uncountable tracers flying by the cockpit. I also hear the groan of the engines as we deliver the weapons, close the bomb bay doors, apply power, and pull up from yet another bomb run on the enemy. The venerable A-26 Invader shudders as we pull up and turn away out of danger, and the two powerful Pratt & Whitney radial engines roar with aggressive determination as we level off and assess the next bomb run. I have flown bombing missions when there was only one bomb run, but the standard combat mission involved multiple bomb runs.

The Nimrods were an indescribable combination of American fighting men. The Nimrod aircrews, maintenance crews and armament crews operated out of Nakhon Phanom RTAFB from 1966 to 1969. I have long resigned myself to knowing that I can never do justice to describing the Nimrods. According to Genesis in the Old Testament, "Nimrod" was "a mighty hunter before the Lord." If you consult a dictionary, the term "Nimrods" means hunters. That is a perfect definition for the combat role we were assigned in the Vietnam War. We were hunters. Each A-26 crew could act as its own Forward Air Controller (FAC), or we could team up with other Forward Air Controllers (air or ground) to locate and strike targets. We often teamed up with FAC aircraft with the call sign Blind Bat or Lamplighter (C-130s), Candlestick (C-123s) and Nail (O-2s). When we flew, our call sign for radio communications was Nimrod and a specified number (e.g., "Nimrod 11" or "Nimrod 24"). Anyone hearing a radio call from someone using a Nimrod call sign instantly knew that an A-26 combat crew was airborne and intent on engaging the enemy.

Incidentally, this story was written forty years after it occurred. My diary written in 1967-68 helped refresh my memory. This is a personal account of the Nimrod story. Time helps us all put things into perspective, and the Vietnam War experience certainly needed time to put things into perspective. The central message from all true warriors is that "we are prepared to fight to the death." The Nimrods were true warriors.

The Nimrod interdiction mission, and the broader Vietnam War experience in general, produced many valuable "lessons learned" that continue to be relevant today.

CHAPTER 2: NIMROD MISSION AND VIETNAM WAR BIG PICTURE

The Nimrod mission in the Vietnam War primarily centered on attacking and destroying enemy truck convoys, troops and supplies as they left North Vietnam, traveled through Laos, and engaged in troop deployment and re-supply operations supporting North Vietnamese (NVN) and Viet Cong (Vietnamese communist) guerilla forces operating in Laos, Cambodia and South Vietnam. The Nimrod armed reconnaissance mission also included combat close air support flight operations in support of U.S. Marines and U.S. Army combat units operating in South Vietnam, and in support of Royal Laotian and Hmong combat units opposing NVN and Pathet Lao (communist) forces in Laos. Nimrod A-26 combat crews operated most often at night, but some missions were flown during daylight hours. Due to the rugged terrain, frequent bad weather and heavy antiaircraft defenses, the nighttime dive-bombing missions were extremely demanding. We routinely teamed up with U.S. forward air controller aircraft, and when possible, we loved to combine air strikes with B-57 (call sign Red Bird and Yellow Bird) strike aircraft. However, on many nights, Nimrod A-26 crews were the only attack combat crews operating in Steel Tiger. Fast movers (e.g., F-4 and F-105 jet fighter bombers) were better suited for operations in North Vietnam, but F-4s sometimes operated at night along the Ho Chi Minh Trail ("Trail"). Occasionally, B-52s conducted concentrated air strikes against key road segments and suspected truck parks. Highly effective A-1E Sandies operated

3

mostly during daytime.

Steel Tiger was the primary area of operations for the Nimrods. Steel Tiger was a military code name for a combat area comprising much of the Ho Chi Minh Trail, a vast network of roads and trails in eastern central Laos extending several hundred miles from North Vietnam north of the Demilitarized Zone (DMZ) south through Laos to South Vietnam and Cambodia. The Ho Chi Minh Trail passed through terrain in Laos that was alternately limestone karst (jutting mountainous terrain), triple-canopy jungle, and grassland. The North Vietnam name for the Trail was the Truong Son Strategic Supply Route (named after the long mountain chain that separates Vietnam from Laos). Historians acknowledge that the Ho Chi Minh Trail was the North Vietnamese lifeline that enabled up to a million NVN troops, and their weapons and war supplies, to reach combat areas in South Vietnam, and that the outcome of the war depended on the infiltration of North Vietnamese troops, weapons, and supplies through Laos into South Vietnam. Until President Nixon acknowledged in 1970 that U.S. aircraft had been, for several years, engaged in flying interdiction missions along the Trail in Laos, the war in Laos was considered by both sides to be the "Secret War in Laos." North Vietnamese government officials such as Prime Minister Pham Van Dong denied in 1966 that North Vietnam was using the Trail in Laos to infiltrate troops and supplies into South Vietnam (after the war he acknowledged that combat forces had been sent down the Trail by the tens of thousands). In the 1960s, the U.S. Government did not want to acknowledge publicly that the war had expanded beyond Vietnam. Beginning in 1966, almost all of the North Vietnamese supply truck convoy activity on the Trail shifted from daylight operations to night operations in an effort to hide from U.S. air strikes. Thereafter, U.S. nighttime strike aircraft, such as A-26, B-57 and C-130 Gunships, became the mainstay of U.S. attack aircraft capability on the Trail. (See generally, Correll, John T., "The Ho Chi Minh Trail," **Air Force Magazine**, November 2005.)[1]

[1] The Air Force Magazine, including back issues, can be accessed online at www. afa.org/magazine/aboutmag.asp.

The Ho Chi Minh Trail stretched hundreds of miles through Laos and Cambodia before terminating in South Vietnam. Mountain passes allowed access to that beleaguered country. (Staff map by Zaur Eylanbekov) (Reprinted by permission from Air Force Magazine, published by the Air Force Association)

Barrel Roll was the other major area of operations for the Nimrods. Barrel Roll covered a very large geographical area in northern Laos, extending from the Plain of Jars eastward to the North Vietnam border. While we only had to fly thirty or forty miles east of Nakhon Phanom (NKP) and the Mekong River to reach the hot combat areas in Steel Tiger, we needed to fly more than 100 miles north just to reach the combat areas in Barrel Roll. Although we didn't give it much thought while we were flying missions, Hanoi was only about 100 miles east of Sam Nua, located in the northeastern part of Barrel Roll. In Steel Tiger, we generally operated from the Mu Gia Pass on the North Vietnam and Laotian border, south past the DMZ, and further south to Saravanne. We also flew combat missions into parts of North Vietnam and South Vietnam adjacent to Steel Tiger and Barrel Roll. The following map of

Laos shows the Barrel Roll and Steel Tiger areas of operation.

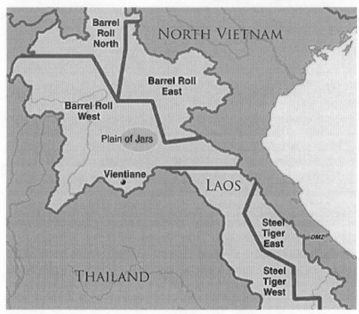

This map shows air operations in Laos. Barrel Roll in northern Laos and Steel Tiger in the south referred both to operations and geographic designations. Steel Tiger East, also called Tiger Hound, was considered an extension of the fight in South Vietnam. Air operations, both south and north, were conducted by 7th Air Force, employing aircraft based in Thailand and South Vietnam. SAC B-52s also operated extensively in Laos. (Staff map by Zaur Eylanbekov) (Reprinted by permission from Air Force Magazine, published by the Air Force Association)

Although the Nimrods engaged in fierce combat on a daily basis (most often at night), the Nimrods were highly disciplined with regard to following the rules of engagement. I cannot remember a single occasion where the rules of engagement were violated. We simply did not bomb villages or civilian noncombatants. We limited our combat operations to military targets and enemy military forces in clearly identified military areas of operation. The Nimrod pilots and navigators were all volunteers. We were career military aviators. We loved flying and we considered it a privilege to serve in the armed forces of the United States of America. We did not shy away from combat. Our sole military purpose, after arriving in the war zone, was to win the war.

Although our sole military purpose was to win the Vietnam War, we were naturally curious about how the United States became involved in the war, and about the big picture concerning military operations in Southeast Asia.

Our understanding was that the United States became involved in the Vietnam War because in the early 1960's the North Vietnamese (led by Ho Chi Minh and General Giap) were not content with communist control only in North Vietnam above the Demilitarized Zone (DMZ); they invaded non-communist South Vietnam below the DMZ and supported Vietnamese communist guerillas (Viet Cong) in an effort to overthrow the South Vietnamese government and forcibly unite North and South Vietnam into a single country under communist control. South Vietnamese government leaders sought military and economic assistance from the United States and Presidents Kennedy, Johnson and Nixon provided that assistance in an effort to preserve an independent and non-communist South Vietnam, and to preclude a feared communist "domino" effect takeover in other countries in Southeast Asia.

We knew that North and South Vietnam had become separate government entities, with a common border at the Demilitarized Zone (DMZ), as a result of the international settlement of the French-Indochina War in 1954. Although France essentially lost that war upon its surrender at Dien Bien Phu on May 7, 1954, nine countries gathered in Geneva, Switzerland to settle the war. Since Ho Chi Minh and the Democratic Republic of Vietnam had defeated the French, they believed that they had a legitimate claim to govern all of Vietnam. However, the major powers at Geneva, including the United States, the Soviet Union and China, backed France's desire for a face-saving exit and divided Vietnam at the seventeenth parallel (i.e., the DMZ). Thus, North Vietnam under Ho Chi Minh became a communist state, and South Vietnam under Ngo Dinh Diem became a separate non-communist state. Thereafter, the Soviet Union and China supported Ho Chi Minh's efforts to conquer all of Vietnam, and the United States supported South Vietnam's efforts to remain an independent non-communist state. According to a 1962 Geneva agreement, Laos was designated a neutral country and all foreign troops were supposed to withdraw from Laos. However, most of the North Vietnamese troops operating in Laos never went home. By the end of 1968, an estimated 40,000 North Vietnamese troops, and an additional 35,000 communist Pathet Lao troops, were engaged in combat operations in Laos. The Nimrods flew armed reconnaissance missions in Laos at the request of the Laotian government. The government of Thailand authorized A-26s to be based at Nakhon Phanom RTAFB, located on the Mekong River in northeast Thailand. As soon as we flew east across the Mekong River, we were in Laos.

From my personal big picture perspective upon arriving in Thailand in late 1967, it appeared that there were three main military areas of operation: South Vietnam (including Cambodia), North Vietnam, and Laos (primarily Steel Tiger and Barrel Roll). U.S. soldiers and South Vietnamese soldiers, supported by U.S. airpower, were heavily involved in fighting against North Vietnamese regulars and communist guerillas in South Vietnam. U.S. airpower (both Air Force and Navy units) were substantially involved in air strikes against military targets in North Vietnam, particularly in the vicinity of Hanoi and Haiphong, but no U.S. soldiers or South Vietnamese soldiers were engaged in ground combat in North Vietnam. The Nimrods were assigned the armed reconnaissance mission of detecting and bombing North Vietnamese trucks and troops as they made their way from North Vietnam down the Ho Chi Minh Trail (in Steel Tiger in central eastern Laos) bound for destinations in South Vietnam and Cambodia. Increasingly in 1968, the Nimrods were assigned armed reconnaissance and close air support missions in support of Royal Laotian and Hmong friendly forces in Barrel Roll in northern Laos. The Nimrods also provided close air support to U.S. Marines at Khe Sanh, located in South Vietnam just south of the DMZ.

CHAPTER 3: THE INCREDIBLE A-26 INVADER

As an Air Force Academy graduate, I had a fairly extensive knowledge of military aircraft, but I had a lot to learn about what makes the A-26 Invader a special aircraft in U.S. military history. The A-26 Invader, an attack bomber, was originally designed and manufactured by the Douglas Aircraft Corporation. A total of 2,446 A-26 aircraft were manufactured by Douglas during World War II. Commander of the Army Air Forces, General H. H. ("Hap") Arnold, was a strong A-26 advocate because he believed the improved performance of the A-26 over its predecessor (the Douglas A-20) would enable the A-26 to replace obsolete A-20, B-25 and B-26 (Martin Marauder) medium bomber aircraft. The new A-26s were first used in combat against the Japanese in the New Guinea campaign during July 1944; however, the A-26s and their crews experienced their greatest test during World War II as the Ninth Air Force flew them into the intense flak environment of central Europe. A-26s (redesignated B-26s in the 1950s) and their crews also saw extensive service flying low-level interdiction missions in the Korean War, and during the Korean conflict were credited with 55,000 combat sorties and the destruction of hundreds of enemy vehicles, railway cars and locomotives. After the Korean War, the Air Force mustered out most of its B-26s, but Invaders proved beneficial once again in a counterinsurgency role during the early part of the Vietnam War.

Early in the Vietnam War (early 1960s), several B-26s and their crews were lost in combat due to wing failure while pulling out of dive-bombing passes. Air Force leaders quickly recognized the renewed valuable role of B-26s in counterinsurgency operations. Design and aging limitations of existing B-26 aircraft led to a 1962 Air Force contract award to On Mark Engineering Company, Van Nuys, California, to develop a prototype YB-26K Counter Invader with structural modifications to strengthen wings and carry additional external ordnance and fuel tanks on the underwing hardpoints. By October 1963, 40 B-26Ks were on order for the Air Force. From the spring of 1966 to November 1969, those 40 B-26Ks were the aircraft flown by Nimrod crews out of Nakhon Phanom RTAFB to bomb, rocket and strafe enemy vehicles, NVN troops and supplies moving down the Ho Chi Minh Trail at night. During the mid-1960s, Thailand did not permit bombers to be based on its soil, resulting in the redesignation of the aircraft to the old attack designation of A-26A. Since operations over Laos could not be publicly acknowledged (the war in Laos was considered "The Secret War"), A-26A combat missions in Southeast Asia remained classified and aircraft national insignia were painted out. In April of 1967, the A-26A Counter Invaders were officially transferred to the 609th Air Commando Squadron (later designated as the 609th Special Operations Squadron in the summer of 1968). Most Nimrod crews simply referred to the aircraft as A-26s or Invaders. Since the On Mark aircraft modifications were such an important contribution to the performance capabilities of the aircraft, the highlights of those modifications are worthy of further elaboration.

The forty A-26A aircraft remanufactured by On Mark Engineering Company in the mid-1960s embodied numerous design and performance improvements. The wings were substantially rebuilt and strengthened by the installation of steel straps on the top and bottom of the spars. Each aircraft was fitted with two Pratt & Whitney 2500 horsepower R-2800-52W water-injected engines with fully reversible automatic feathering propellers. Wing-tip fuel tanks (165 gallon capacity each) were permanently installed at the tip of each wing. Eight new underwing pylons were added to carry various munitions and stores. Eight .50 caliber forward-firing machine guns were added to the aircraft nose section. The rudder was enlarged and an anti-skid wheel braking system was installed. The instrument panel was revised and dual flight controls were provided in the cockpit. The top and sides of each aircraft was painted in a dark green jungle camouflage pattern, and the bottom of each aircraft was painted black. The On Mark A-26A modifications increased the maximum cruising speed from 240 to 265 knots, the combat radius from 210 to 500 nautical miles, and increased the armament load from 7,500 to 12,000 pounds.

Without the crucial On Mark modifications, Nimrod crews could not have carried out demanding dive-bombing missions over the Ho Chi Minh Trail. Equally as important to the mission, the On Mark modifications enabled Nimrod crews to carry vastly improved loads of munitions and flares. A-26A aircraft could carry up to 8000 pounds of munitions and stores on the eight pylon wing stations; 4000 pounds of bombs in the internal bomb bay; and eight .50 caliber machine guns and ammunition in the nose of the aircraft. In 1966 and early 1967, a typical underwing load for a combat mission included a pair of SUU-025 flare dispensers, two LAU-3A rocket pods, and four CBU-14 cluster bomb unit containers. As combat operations over the Ho Chi Minh Trail intensified in 1967, the flares and rockets were often replaced with 500-pound BLU-23, or 750-pound BLU-27, finned napalm bombs. Nimrod crews also recognized the importance of modifications enabling highly effective bomb loads of 500 pound M-31 and M-32 incendiary bomb clusters, M-34 and M-35 incendiary bombs, M1A4 fragmentation bomb clusters, M-47 white phosphorus bombs, and CBU-24 and various other cluster bomb units. General-purpose bombs (e.g., 250-pound MK81, 500-pound MK82, and 750-pound MK117 bombs) could also be carried. The extensive munitions carrying capability of the aircraft, combined with the eight .50 caliber machine guns in the aircraft nose, made the A-26A Invader a most formidable aircraft weapons system.

Following the On Mark modifications, as reported at the website of the National Museum of the USAF,[2] the Air Force revised the Douglas B-26K (A-26A) Counter Invader specifications and performance as follows:

---

[2] www.nationalmuseum.af.mil/factsheets/factsheet.asp?id=301

SPECIFICATIONS:
Wing Span: 71 ft. 6 in.
Length: 51 ft. 7 in.
Height: 19 ft.
Weight: 38,314 lbs. maximum
Armament: Eight .50 cal. nose guns (2800 rounds of ammunition when fully loaded), eight wing pylons capable of carrying 8000 lbs. of mixed ordnance, and 4000 lbs. of bombs internally
Engines: Two Pratt & Whitney R-2800-52Ws of 2500 hp (maximum with water injection)
Crew: Two
Cost: $577,000

PERFORMANCE:
Maximum Speed: 323 mph/281 knots
Range: 2700 statute miles/2346 nautical miles
Service Ceiling: 30,000 ft.

When I reported for A-26 training in 1967 at England Air Force Base, Alexandria, Louisiana, I was subjected to a lot of kidding by veteran A-26 pilots and navigators because it was highly unusual for a B-52 crewmember to transition from a jet strategic nuclear bombing mission to a prop tactical dive-bombing mission. I must admit that the A-26 looked quite strange to me the first time I saw one at England Air Force Base. However, I quickly became a big fan of the A-26; it was a pure joy to fly!

My role in A-26s was very different from my role in B-52s. In B-52s I sat beside another navigator-bombardier in the "basement" of the aircraft surrounded by radarscopes and navigation and bombing instruments. In the A-26, I sat in the cockpit in the right seat (beside the pilot who occupied the left seat) and I functioned as both a navigator and co-pilot (my bombardier training also fit the new mission). Suddenly I was out of the basement and in the right seat of the cockpit with a full view outside the canopy. Also, like the pilot, I had a full set of flight controls, and the throttle, RPM and mixture controls were positioned between the pilot and co-pilot seats. Officially, I held navigator, bombardier, and parachutist ratings. Unofficially, the A-26 pilots we flew with trained the right-seat navigators to also become proficient co-pilots. The A-26 pilot's primary job was to fly the airplane, and bomb and strafe targets (using the bomb sight in front of the pilot). The navigator's primary job was to navigate, perform co-pilot duties, and manage the fuel system and the armament and bombing systems. Both crewmembers shared radio communication duties and good crew coordination was of utmost importance. When we were recommended for awards and decorations, pilots were referred to as A-26 Attack Bomber Pilots and navigators were referred to as A-26 Attack Bomber Navigator/Co-Pilots. Flying the A-26 was a real flying by the "seat of your pants" experience. We felt a special kinship with each other, and with A-26 crews that flew combat missions in World War II and the Korean War. I loved the new role.

CHAPTER 4: AIR FORCE BACKGROUND PRIOR TO A-26 ASSIGNMENT

In 1967, when I first heard that I had an assignment to an A-26 Air Commando Squadron, I was serving as a navigator on a B-52 crew at Loring Air Force Base, Maine. I had completed navigator-bombardier training and B-52 crew training only a couple of years earlier in California, and I had just been selected to fly as a navigator on one of our B-52 Stand Board crews (enforce tough flight standards). It was a strange time for Air Force crews and their families. My wife, Dianne, and I were married in 1963 and our only daughter at the time, Kimberly, was only two years old. Dianne and I had expected to be at Loring for at least four years. Some of the crewmembers had been there eight years. However, the war changed all that. A lot of crewmembers in our B-52 squadron were being notified of assignments to Southeast Asia at the time. When I unexpectedly received word of the A-26 assignment, I was somewhat dumbfounded because I didn't really know what kind of aircraft and unit I had been assigned to, and I didn't really expect to receive a new assignment to a different aircraft after being a B-52 crewmember for only two years. However, most interesting as I think back on it, one of my veteran B-52 radar-navigator friends obviously knew exactly what the A-26 aircraft and assignment were all about because he congratulated me on being a young "tiger" for taking on the A-26 assignment. Although we certainly had some apprehension about the new assignment and what the future might bring, Dianne and I packed up in the summer of 1967 and moved to

Alexandria, Louisiana, where the A-26 training was to take place.

Dianne and I started dating in high school and we were married on October 26, 1963, the fall after she graduated from Concord College (now Concord University) and I graduated from the Air Force Academy. Dianne became a career teacher and Super Mom and I became a career military officer. As members of the teaching and military professions, Dianne and I always had a purpose bigger than ourselves, and I was always blessed to have her unwavering support no matter what challenges we faced.

The four-year (1959-63) experience as a cadet at the Air Force Academy in Colorado Springs, Colorado had a huge impact on my life. I was most fortunate to have obtained a nomination from Congresswoman Elizabeth Kee to attend the Academy upon graduation from high school. The Academy placed strong emphasis on military training, discipline, academics, and physical fitness through exercise programs and sports. The Academy also emphasized honor, ethics, integrity and an undying sense of patriotism. Most of my 1963 classmates served in Vietnam. The Academy was our foundation. Flight school gave us the technical skills. When we received news of our assignments in the Vietnam War, we were ready. The support of our families was of vital importance to us. Our core values were and are…"Duty, Honor, Country." We formed strong personal bonds during our Academy years that go far beyond mere friendship. We know what it means to be a "Band of Brothers." I have stayed in contact with my classmates from the First Cadet Squadron throughout the years. The core group of my Academy classmates include: John Borling, Grant Bornzin, Dave Byrne, Merrill Eastcott, Stu Fenske, Jim Fausey, Cliff Haney, Bob Hanneken, Joe Hanes, Bill Heinlein, Rob Mahoney, C. L. Melenyzer, Pete Ognibene, Jack Ott, George Pasquet, Jack Pierson, Gene Rosendahl, Mick Roth, Dave Rotz, Glen Shaffer, Mike Tomme, Gary Wallace and Gary West. I didn't realize it at the time, but my A-26 Nimrod assignment introduced me to a second "Band of Brothers."

CHAPTER 5: A-26 TRAINING IN LOUISIANA AND FLORIDA

After initial aircraft transition training at England AFB, we quickly spent most of our time on the bombing range where we practiced day-after-day improving our crew coordination in dive bombing and strafing attack techniques. With my B-52 background, I wasn't used to all of the abrupt, turning dives into the target, and pulling Gs as we pulled off the target in sharp, climbing turns. My biggest challenge was keeping my breakfast down when we made strafing runs on the target range. During the strafing runs, the eight .50 caliber machine guns in the nose section of the aircraft were blazing away and the cockpit filled up with smoke from the machine guns…combine the nauseating smoke with constant turns, dives and climb-outs and you have a perfect recipe for throwing up. I did just that on more than one occasion.

It was during A-26 training at England AFB that I met one of the central characters of my Vietnam War experience. That man was Major Bobby Joe Sears of Dallas, Texas. Major Sears was a pilot and I instantly liked his style. He was full of life and he impressed me as an outstanding pilot. He was probably in his mid-30s at the time but he had a fair amount of premature gray hair. Everybody called him "Pappy." The nickname stuck. I remember approaching Pappy in a briefing room at England AFB and asking him if he would like to team up as a crew. It was my good fortune that he said "yes." To finish our training, we flew a cross-county flight from England AFB to Hurlburt Field, Florida. I still remember flying low-level across the rolling terrain of northern Alabama in October of 1967. The leaves were at the peak of their autumn glory. We flew with live bombs for the first time on the bombing ranges in Florida. I still vividly remember our first nighttime napalm drop on the bombing range near Eglin AFB, Florida. The night was black but the whole sky lit up behind us as we released the napalm and pulled off the bombing pass. In November of 1967, we were pronounced ready for duty in Southeast Asia.

CHAPTER 6: IMPORTANCE OF FAMILY AND PAIN OF SEPARATION

The importance of family to military personnel cannot be overstated. All too soon, the time for A-26 training came to an end and it was time to say goodbye to Dianne and Kimberly ("Kim"). Dianne decided to live with her mother in Princeton, West Virginia during the year that I would be away at Nakhon Phanom RTAFB, Thailand. I still have strong memories of the early morning hours on November 19, 1967, when it was time for me to leave Dianne and Kim. I remember visiting Kim's bed in the early morning light and giving her a goodbye kiss as she slept. She was only two years old and looked like a beautiful little angel. After saying a prayer at Kim's bedside, Dianne and I drove to the Mercer County Airport so that I could catch my flight. I remember being in my Air Force "Class-A Blues" uniform (with tie and silver wings), and I remember how painful it was for both Dianne and me to say goodbye. I also remember tears rolling down my face as the aircraft took off and turned west toward California.

Dianne and I first met when my family moved to Athens, West Virginia, in the summer of 1954. I was twelve and Dianne was eleven. She says that she fell in love with me the first time she saw me on the outdoor basketball playground at the start of school that year. I believe her. Dianne was and is a remarkable woman. She knows who she is and she knows what she wants. My first recollection of Dianne is that she was very attractive and very determined. I can still remember her riding her bike with friends in Athens in 1954. At eleven years

19

of age she had a full head of dark brown hair in long rolls that fell well below her shoulders. She was athletic and she had a mischievous but very determined look in her eyes. She had a prominent "British" nose and a bright expression in her eyes, and she looked like someone you would expect to see somewhere in England or Ireland. She was strikingly beautiful. Not only that, she was probably the brightest and most industrious student in the entire school. She was and is the only girl and woman that I ever loved. Even in 1954, I realized that I was a complete rookie concerning the realm of romance, but I also realized that there was something very special about that very determined young lady. In short, much to my eternal good fortune, I had been had. We didn't really begin dating until high school. I played basketball in high school and Dianne was a cheerleader. It was a wonderful time to be a teenager in America. We were thrilled to win the state high school basketball tournament in 1959 when I was a senior and Dianne was a junior. It was very much like "Happy Days" on TV. We continued dating in college and after college graduation were married on October 26, 1963, at Laredo AFB, Texas.

Classmates and good friends (John Borling, Bob Hanneken, Gary Wallace, and Cliff Haney) from the Air Force Academy were our sword bearers. Cliff Haney was my Best Man and Sue Hanneken was Dianne's Matron of Honor. I can still see Dianne coming down the aisle in the wedding chapel! I was happy but nervous and somewhat stunned! I could not have hoped for a more beautiful bride!!! She wore a gorgeous white wedding dress and she was absolutely radiant as she walked down the aisle and smiled at me as we turned toward the chaplain for the wedding vows. We honeymooned in Nuevo Laredo, Mexico, and Kimberly was born two years later while I was in navigator-bombardier training at Sacramento, California. Dianne and I had only been married four years when it was time for me to leave for combat duty in the Vietnam War in 1967. Personal involvement in the Vietnam War was a rude awakening for all of us! I had drastically underestimated how painful it would be to leave Dianne and Kimberly and depart for combat duty in Thailand. I know that it was just as painful for Dianne.

CHAPTER 7: JUNGLE SURVIVAL TRAINING AND ARRIVAL IN THAILAND

As an Air Force crewmember, it seemed very strange to me to fly to war in commercial aircraft. After leaving West Virginia, my commercial flights took me to California and Alaska before arriving in the Philippines for jungle survival training. Upon arrival at Clark Air Base in the Philippines, I immediately observed a bus full of wounded U.S. military personnel en route to U.S. hospitals from the Southeast Asia battlefield. It seemed that everyone was covered head-to-toe in white bandages. They had a pained expression in their eyes. That chance encounter left no doubt that I was beginning to approach the combat zone of the Vietnam War.

Jungle survival school lasted approximately one week. It was an amazing experience. I had previously completed aircrew survival school at Stead Air Force Base, Nevada before becoming part of a B-52 crew, but this was different. The essence of the training was being exposed to the jungle and the natives who lived there. I had never seen tropical plants, trees, insects and animals up close until jungle survival school. It was a sobering experience for Americans because we had never had to confront our fears about the jungle before. During the last night of the training, I was teamed with another Air Force crewmember and our assignment was to escape and evade the native Negritos whose assigned role was to find and capture us at night. To my surprise, the Negritos were small black natives who actually still lived in thatched huts in the lush tropical forests of the Philippines. We soon found out that they

21

were experts in the tropical and mountain environment. Growing up in West Virginia, I had spent much of my youth hunting, fishing and camping in the Appalachian Mountains. I loved the great outdoors, so I thought I had a shot at evading the natives. Wrong! Even though my buddy and I sought out the most obscure ravine we could find in the middle of the night in a remote part of the Philippines, the Negritos discovered us before dawn. They approached us so quietly that we didn't know they were there until they reached out and touched us. I heard that they could actually smell Americans, and that they were given a bag of rice for every American they found at night. They must have stocked up on rice for weeks, because I don't remember a single American crewmember avoiding detection. I do remember one American yelling and screaming in the middle of the night because a large spider had crawled into his sleeping bag.

Needless to say, we were happy to graduate from jungle survival school and continue on our way to Bangkok. Our last commercial flight on our journey landed at Don Muang Air Base located on the outskirts of Bangkok. After we departed the aircraft, the entire scene was converted to a bustling military operation. Everywhere we looked there were long lines of military personnel in camouflage uniforms, green flying suits, or jungle fatigues. After staying overnight in modest quarters, I boarded a C-130 tactical airlift aircraft early the next morning at Don Muang, and I sat in web seating in the passenger area of the aircraft for the flight to Nakhon Phanom Royal Thai Air Force Base, a flight lasting a few hours. The C-130 impressed me as being a loud and powerful airplane. The four large turboprop engines roared, and the aircraft shook and vibrated as we lifted off the runway. There was no doubt that we had left the world of smooth commercial jet travel, and that we were approaching the war zone. I will never forget my first look at Nakhon Phanom Royal Thai Air Force Base as the C-130 flew over the field before turning and landing. As I looked down from approximately 3000 feet altitude, there were prop aircraft everywhere sending clouds of dust into the air. The nearby green tropical trees were swaying wildly from the intense prop wash. I could make out the A-26 parking area, and large numbers of single-engine fighter aircraft, transports, and helicopters. NKP (the nickname for Nakhon Phanom Royal Thai Air Force Base), located in northeast Thailand, lay adjacent to the Mekong River and Laos. It was obviously a strategic location to wage the Vietnam War for prop aircraft and their crews. After landing, I was quickly escorted to my quarters (a two-man trailer) and I was very happy to rejoin Bobby Sears and the rest of the Nimrod squadron.

This is an aerial view of Nakhon Phanom Royal Thai Air Force Base, Thailand looking from South to North (circa 1967-69). The active runway is on the far left and the U.S. forces lived in right center.

CHAPTER 8: LIFE AT NKP

Life at NKP was very much like living in a Wild West gold rush town. There was non-stop combat flight activity, and the hectic pace of life on the base reminded me of a gold rush town I had seen in the movies. If you were on the flight line, prop aircraft were busily taking off, landing, or taxiing to or from the main runway, and there was a constant bustle of aircraft maintenance and armament activity going on 24 hours-a-day, seven days a week. Since I had come from a B-52 base in the States, it was quite a sight to see large numbers of A-26, A-1E, T-28, C-130, C-123, P-2V and O-2 aircraft, and many types of helicopters, operating on an around-the-clock basis. Many of those aircraft were either shot down or shot up during my tour. I marveled at how much antiaircraft damage the aircraft could take and still make it back to NKP. I distinctly remember seeing a basketball-size hole extending completely through the rear fuselage of an A-1E parked at NKP. Jet aircraft were assigned at other military airfields in Thailand, but we only had prop aircraft assigned at NKP. The control tower dominated the skyline on the western side of NKP. If you looked toward the east, you saw the ominous outline of the mountains in the Steel Tiger area of Laos. Off to the side of the airfield, a secure large ordnance area stored vast quantities of munitions that were consumed daily by the strike aircraft. The business side of life at NKP involved absolute devotion to duty, which meant that Air Force personnel did whatever it took to keep our combat aircraft airborne and in pursuit of the enemy around-the-clock. For NKP strike aircraft, the A-26 Nimrods ruled the night—the A-1E Sandies ruled the day.

There was another side to life at NKP away from the flight line. When I arrived at NKP in November of 1967, I saw a medium-sized base that was still growing rapidly. Air Force "Red Horse" engineering and construction personnel were everywhere building everything from barracks to military headquarters to medical units. Almost all of the buildings were wood structures, and most of the streets were unpaved. We had an Officers' Club, a Non-Commissioned Officers' Club, a post office, a military exchange store, a softball field, and even a basic movie theater. Receiving mail from home was crucial for our morale. Dianne's letters meant the world to me. The military exchange store permitted us to buy a top quality stereo system at a reasonable price. I loved my TEAC tape deck and my record turntable. We regularly exchanged favorite records and tapes. We also formed a great softball league—each squadron fielded a team and we loved the games and the competition. We also enjoyed seeing movies in our no-frills movie theater. To a great extent, life for Nimrod crews at NKP centered on our two-man trailers, the O' Club and the Nimrod patio.

This photo shows the Base Exchange store (right foreground) and other base buildings at Nakhon Phanom Royal Thai Air Force Base (NKP) in 1968. (Photo is from Frank Nelson collection.)

The two-man trailers didn't look like much, but they were a Godsend for combat crews. Bobby Sears and I shared one of those two-man trailers. Each of us had a bed and a desk in rooms on opposite sides of the trailer. A bathroom separated the two rooms. After we had flown a night mission, we could cover the windows, lock the doors, and turn day into night for a "night's" sleep.

Photo shows the Nimrod two-man trailer crew quarters at NKP (1967-69).
(Photo is from Frank Nelson collection.)

The small trailers were our homes. That is where I retreated to read Dianne's letters. That is where I retreated to listen to music on my stereo system and do some reading. That is where I read, for the first time, the entire Bible. As a Christian, reading the Bible gave me great strength.

Away from the flight line and our trailers, you could almost always find us hanging out at either the O' Club or the Nimrod patio. The O' Club was the main social center for all of the officers at NKP. The Nimrod patio was a special gathering place for Nimrod crews. For exercise, we loved the softball competition.

Photo shows one of many Nimrod softball games at NKP in 1968. Pappy Sears is the pitcher for the Nimrods and Roger Graham is playing shortstop. Unfortunately, identity of Nimrod player in outfield is unknown. (Photo is from Frank Nelson collection.)

If NKP was a great Wild West gold rush town, the O' Club was our grand saloon. I can't even begin to tell you what all went on at the NKP O' Club. But I will try. I will start out tame. The O' Club is where we met for drinks and breakfast after yet another mission into Steel Tiger or Barrel Roll. You could either go directly to the breakfast area, or you could toss down a few at the bar and then go to the breakfast area. The tempo of the combat mission you had just flown seemed to help you decide which choice to make. Our first choice was almost always to go directly to the bar. But, I said I am starting out tame. On those occasions when we went directly to the dining area, a gracious Thai staff and excellent food were waiting for us. On those occasions when we went to the bar first, we were met by a room full of crewmembers in flight suits fresh off a mission, and you could count on hearing all of the latest war stories from a wild and crazy bunch of American combat crewmembers who had just survived another mission. The noise level was deafening!

No matter what time of day or night, one song seemed to always be playing on the sound system at the O' Club. That song was "San Francisco (Be Sure to Wear Some Flowers in Your Hair)." I loved that song. I believe that every member of the Air Force at NKP loved that song. To us, it was a beautiful song that gave us hope that some day we might get to return to the United States of America and to the people we loved. The song made it to the Top Ten in the States, but it made it to Number One on the charts for all of us at NKP. The lyrics and music were beautiful, haunting and unforgettable: "If you're going to San Francisco, be sure to wear some flowers in your hair; if you're going to San Francisco, you're gonna meet some gentle people there…." We never got tired of hearing that incredibly beautiful song.

The bar at the NKP O' Club was a place where combat crews depressurized after yet another life-or-death mission. For that reason, commanders cut the crews a little slack at the O' Club bar. Imagine the scene. You have just made multiple night dive-bombing passes on a convoy of trucks at the Mu Gia Pass in Steel Tiger, survived ten or more AAA guns hammering away at you, survived close mid-air collisions and survived close encounters with the ground when pulling up from dive-bombing passes, and much to your relief, you have survived yet another mission and you are back in the O' Club bar at

NKP. Naturally, you are damn happy to still be alive! Naturally, you want to raise a little hell! The NKP bar let you do that. You could have any type of drink you wanted. You could arm-wrestle, leg-wrestle, throw your buddy over the bar, shout, tell war stories, and throw empty drink glasses. You could do just about anything short of hurting or killing your fellow airmen and soldiers. That is where we drew the line. Two of my most vivid recollections at the NKP bar involved a female officer leg-wrestling a male officer on the bar floor in the middle of the night (female officer won), and Captain Don Maxwell, Nimrod navigator/co-pilot and officer and gentleman extraordinaire, driving his motorcycle into the O' Club and bar in the wee hours of yet another memorable night at the good old NKP O' Club bar! The O' Club also permitted you to play poker to your heart's content. In short, the O' Club was a safe haven that allowed us to depressurize after flying yet another life-threatening combat mission. The next day, the combat cycle started all over again.

The Nimrod patio was another central gathering place for Nimrod crews. The Nimrod patio did not exist when I first reported to NKP in November of 1967. When I reported to NKP, we had about twenty two-man trailers housing our A-26 crews. But then a wonderful thing happened. Captain Frank Nelson, an A-26 navigator, somehow appeared with an engineering design for an outdoor patio area suitable for about fifty people. It was a perfect design for a squadron of our size. The design included a screened-in building with an adjoining BBQ pit. Other than an O' Club, what more could a flight squadron want? Under Frank's calm and expert guidance, we zealously tackled the Nimrod patio project. In no time at all, the beams, walls, and doors were in place, the roof was constructed, the screen windows were stretched and tacked, the BBQ pit was built, and we were in business! The Nimrod patio was located in the middle of our two-man trailers and it quickly became a natural hangout for all Nimrod crews. We enjoyed many squadron BBQ cookouts with everyone in attendance. Even more important to me personally, I can remember countless nights and early morning hours when I would join other Nimrods for a beer and companionship at the patio. My good friends, Leroy (Roy) Zarucchi, Robert (Zim) Zimmerman, Richard (Dick) Willems, and Larry Counts and I met there often to discuss the topic of the night, the highlights of our latest missions, and the madness of war. Many times we were joined by other Nimrods. We knew it was time to go to bed when the big red Sun in the hazy low eastern sky started rising above the lower sections of the patio screened windows.

Photo shows Nimrod Patio constructed by A-26 flight crews shortly before completion of construction in 1968. Success equals good design plus good teamwork. (Photo is from Frank Nelson collection)

On a couple of occasions, to relieve stress and break the normal routine, I joined a group of Nimrod friends for a bus trip into the local town of Nakhon Phanom to play tourist and enjoy a Thai dinner. We only did that during daylight hours. We were mindful that a war was going on and that Takhet, Laos lay just across the Mekong River from the town of Nakhon Phanom. Some of our military operations took place not too far from Takhet (sometimes spelled Thakhek), so we knew there was a possibility that some enemy infiltrators could be present in Nakhon Phanom. Thankfully, our rare dinner trips were peaceful.

I recall the bus trip of about ten miles on a dusty, dirt road from the base to the town. The town of Nakhon Phanom (also referred to as NKP City) had a population of approximately 16,000 people in 1967-68. Most of the business section of the town lay on or near the Mekong River. The roads and streets were all unpaved. I recall seeing numerous palm trees, and various tropical plants and flowers.

The river was wide and the temperature was warm. With the Mekong River backdrop, the towns of Nakhon Phanom, Thailand and Takhet, Laos were quite picturesque.

Laos across the Mekong from NKP City.

View of the rugged mountains in Laos across the Mekong River from Nakhon Phanom, Thailand.

The people we encountered on the streets seemed preoccupied with their own lives and didn't seem to be concerned about our presence. We visited the same Thai restaurant during each visit. I don't recall the name of the restaurant but I do recall a water buffalo lumbering on the dirt street outside the restaurant during one visit. The water buffalo had an impressive set of horns, but he didn't seem interested in us. We gave him plenty of space. The restaurant special was Kobe steak with Thai vegetables. The dinner was excellent and the staff was friendly and efficient. After an enjoyable dinner, we boarded the bus for the short trip back to the base. I still wonder what all might have been going on in the town of Nakhon Phanom that remained hidden to us.

The stress of combat flying does take its toll. I remember one occasion late in my combat tour when I had flown a night combat mission, attended the de-briefings, and stayed up the rest of the night because I had some work I needed to do at the squadron that morning. I remember visiting my good friend Major Robert Zimmerman ("Zim") in the hospital, walking to the post office in the early morning hours to see if I had received a letter from Dianne, and then walking to the small bank building on base to deposit some money. For some reason, the door to the bank slammed closed on one of my fingers. That is all it took. I was suffering from overstress and fatigue. The moment the door slammed on my finger, the lights went out and I hit the deck. I remember the jolting pain, and I remember collapsing and the start of the fall to the floor. I do not remember hitting the floor. I revived soon afterward with about ten Thais (bank employees) rubbing my back, arms and neck. It was really embarrassing to have to explain all of this to the Fight Surgeon, who told me not to fly that night and to go to bed. Bobby Sears and John Shippey (who became our squadron commander shortly thereafter) obviously understood what had happened. I took some kidding, but it was good-natured kidding. They gave me a day off to recover and I was back on the flight schedule with a sore finger two nights later. I flew with an unforgettable group of Nimrod pilots and navigators, and we flew many unforgettable missions. I would like to attempt to describe some of those unforgettable Nimrods and missions for you.

CHAPTER 9:
UNFORGETTABLE NIMRODS
AND A-26 COMBAT
MISSIONS (PART I)

The unforgettable Nimrod pilots and navigators of the 609th Air Commando Squadron were some of the most diverse personality types I had ever encountered, and many of the high-intensity dive-bombing combat missions we flew were equally unforgettable. It seemed that every pilot and navigator had a unique but strong personality. The extreme stress of combat was shared by all, but the reactions to the stress brought out different personality traits from different individuals. We all wanted to win, and we gave everything we had toward that winning effort. There were some forty pilots and navigators in our squadron at any given point in time. We quickly became a band of brothers that had complete faith and confidence in each other. Our collective mentality was attack and win. I will attempt to describe some of the more memorable missions.

a. **First Combat Zone Familiarization Mission with Carlos and Bill**

I can remember it like it was yesterday. I was fresh from duty as a B-52 navigator-bombardier. I had just completed A-26 training at England Air Force Base, Alexandria, Louisiana, and Jungle Survival School at Clark Air Base in the Philippines. The date was December

4, 1967. It was nighttime—the throttles were pushed full forward and we were racing down the runway. Captain Carlos Cruz was in the left seat and Captain Bill Potter was in the right seat. I was sitting in the "jump seat" behind Bill Potter as Carlos and Bill advanced the throttles. Everything seemed routine as we lifted off, made a climbing left turn toward the east, and leveled off at about 7000 feet. We continued to drone eastward as Carlos and Bill searched for targets and chattered on the radio. I was trying to take it all in but I was oblivious to what was really happening. All at once, Carlos and Bill shouted that we were attacking a target. Immediately, the aircraft, and all of us, were propelled into a steep dive attacking the targets below. The bombs were released. There was a bright illumination as the bombs detonated upon impact. I remember the hosing of tracers to the front, side, and rear of the aircraft as we made repeated passes attacking the targets and recovering to a safe altitude. I especially remember multiple bursts of reddish-colored tracers flashing by the rear of our aircraft every time we completed a pass and abruptly pulled up and turned away from the target. Think of a pitch-black scene where numerous spurts of antiaircraft tracers almost blast you and your aircraft out of the sky. First you are in a screaming dive into the darkness, and then you are immediately slammed back into your seat as the aircraft pulls up and turns away from the bomb run. At the same time, tracers are flying by your cockpit and bright illuminations fill the sky as the bombs strike the ground. That was the scene. I didn't fully comprehend what was happening, but I wanted to believe that I would survive whatever was happening.

After the agony of repeated bombing attacks, we somehow survived and returned to a safe altitude and flew west until we landed at Nakhon Phanom RTAFB (NKP), Thailand. I can never forget the pre-flight of that mission. I vividly recall walking around the aircraft during the pre-flight inspection. I also clearly recall walking under the open bomb bay of the aircraft with Carlos inspecting the bombs and telling me that he and Bill would like to be awarded a Silver Star. Carlos and Bill had flown more than 100 combat missions at that point in time. From the jump seat behind the co-pilot seat, I flew my first combat mission in the Vietnam War. When we were in the Steel Tiger area, we repeatedly dive-bombed targets of opportunity, streams of tracers raced by the cockpit, and I was totally mesmerized by what was happening. Carlos was unbelievably aggressive, both verbally and physically, as he and Bill attacked the enemy below in pass after pass. Bill was unbelievably calm and stoic in all of the chaos, seemingly in perfect harmony with Carlos, the ordnance delivery systems, and the flow of the mission. Somehow, we survived. Somehow, we entered the landing pattern at NKP, and somehow, we landed and walked away from that aircraft. I was amazed. I still remember them kidding me about being a B-52 navigator-bombardier, and about me being pale as a ghost. All preconceived notions had just been totally erased. I now knew that there really was a war going on in Southeast Asia. My last notation in my diary for that date was: "It's going to be a very long year...I hope!"

b. The Silver Star Mission with Dick Schramm

I checked my One Year Diary and was surprised to notice that Major Dick Schramm and I flew our Silver Star mission on December 20, 1967. That was only my eleventh combat mission in the Vietnam War. I was still green behind the ears. Not true for Dick Schramm. He flew like a demon possessed. But, I am getting ahead of myself. As I look back, I have no idea why I appeared on the flight schedule to fly with Dick Schramm that night. That is one of the few flights that we ever flew together. The explanation must have been that I was deemed combat-ready after my seventh mission on December 15, and Pappy and I didn't start flying again as a crew until December 23. For whatever reason, Dick Schramm's regularly assigned navigator/co-pilot was not available to fly on the night of December 20, and I got the nod. I recall that Dick Schramm was a Major and a seasoned pilot. He was somewhat short, about 5' 9," medium but powerful build, hair somewhat thinning in front, seasoned flight suit, large bigger-than-life-eyes, big forehead, ready to laugh at the world—but at the same time—all business. I had my hands full just keeping up with him.

Checking my diary, I notice that I didn't get out of bed until two o'clock in the afternoon on December 20, 1967. That wasn't so unusual because we normally flew at all hours of the night. For some reason, I felt exhausted all day. That was unusual for a young man twenty-five years of age. Oddly, the Bob Hope Show appeared at an outdoor stage at NKP the night before. It was a great show! The show included movie actress Raquel Welch and the Les Brown Band. Bob Hope was always a great supporter of U.S. military personnel assigned overseas at Christmas, and we cheered wildly after every wisecrack Bob made about Naked Fannie (NKP). Maybe staying up late after the show left me exhausted, or maybe it was the stress of adjusting to combat. After Dick Schramm and I attended the pre-flight briefings on the night of December 20, I remember feeling weak as I climbed up the ladder leading to the cockpit. However, I was committed to fly at that point. I soon had my reserve adrenalin pumping because it was an unusually hot mission.

No sooner had we climbed out and leveled off than we were directed by Alley Cat, the C-130 Airborne Command and Control Center (ABCCC) aircraft, to fly immediately to one of the hottest areas of the Ho Chi Minh Trail. Dick Schramm proved himself to be an outstanding combat pilot that night. He flawlessly worked us into the attack pattern and delivered pass after pass of ordnance on the truck convoy below. I remember doing everything that I had been trained to do and doing it in unison with my left-seater who obviously knew what he was doing. We made attack after attack. I remember the tracers flying all around our aircraft and I remember repeated flashes as our bombs detonated on trucks on the road structure below. I particularly remember being in 60 degree nose-down dive attitudes and trading our mix of ordnance with at least six enemy gunners in scattered positions who were firing 23-millimeter (ZPU) and 37-millimeter rounds directly at us. The tracers coming at us were white hot and red hot and appeared to be accelerating directly into my face. Dick never faltered. He instinctively evaded the antiaircraft fire and hit the enemy where it hurt. Although this was the first time we had flown together, we methodically dropped or fired every type of ordnance we had at the enemy. We could see that we were hitting trucks and we could see that we were hitting antiaircraft gun positions. In the thick of battle, you don't stop until you are out of firepower. When we were finally out of ordnance, we leveled off and checked out with the FAC and Alley Cat and headed home. After the flight I literally collapsed in bed back at NKP.

Several months later, I learned that Dick Schramm and I had been awarded Silver Stars for the mission on the night of December 20, 1967. I didn't know we had been recommended for a decoration. The official records credited us with the destruction of one 37-millimeter antiaircraft gun, three trucks destroyed, and over nine tons of supplies and equipment destroyed. In addition, the FAC credited us with sixteen secondary fires and three secondary explosions. We were conservative with our bomb damage assessments. We didn't count a truck destroyed unless it burned on the Trail. The Silver Star is awarded for gallantry in action. It is a prized military decoration for combat service. I am honored that I was awarded the Silver Star, and I am certain that Dick Schramm must feel the same way. That was a real shoot-out at the OK corral—we dived directly into the teeth of enemy fire and saw our firepower knock them out before they could shoot us out of the sky. We could do no more.

Many Nimrods were awarded Silver Stars for similar missions over the Ho Chi Minh Trail. I believe that all Nimrods who flew those missions deserved Silver Stars.

My recollection is that the 609th Air Commando Squadron (later renamed the 609th Special Operations Squadron) had the honor of being awarded at least two Presidential Unit Citations. The Presidential Unit Citation is awarded to units of the Armed Forces of the United States for extraordinary heroism in action against an armed enemy occurring on or after December 7, 1941. The unit must display such gallantry, determination, and esprit de corps in accomplishing its mission under extremely difficult and hazardous conditions as to set it apart and above other units participating in the same campaign. The degree of heroism required is the same as that which would warrant award of a Distinguished Service Cross to an individual. Extended periods of combat duty or participation in a large number of operational missions, either ground or air is not sufficient. This award is normally earned by units that have participated in single or successive actions covering relatively brief time spans. It is not reasonable to presume that entire units can sustain Distinguished Service Cross performance for extended time periods except under the most unusual circumstances.

c. The Christmas Night Mission

As Christmas Eve approached, the Nimrods took time to reflect on the meaning of Christmas, and to remember our loved ones back home. I felt like I had gotten over the initial hurdle of adjusting to life at NKP, but it certainly felt very strange living in a jungle setting in Thailand during the Christmas season. About a week before Christmas, I was very thankful to receive a package from Dianne that contained three Christmas presents. The Christmas presents were like *treasure* to me. I carefully placed each present on the makeshift desk in my room and knew that I would not think of opening them until Christmas morning. I'm sure that every member of the Nimrods felt the same way. Nothing was better than receiving a letter or a package from your wife back home. That is what we fought for, and that is what we lived for. I'm sure it has always been the same for all soldiers in all wars. You live, fight, and sometimes die for the ones you love.

Christmas Eve, December 24, 1967, was a special, melancholy time. I had flown my thirteenth combat mission on the night of December 23 with Major Bobby Sears, which happened to be the first time we had flown together as a crew in Thailand. It was great flying with "Pappy" again. I *really* liked Pappy. I really liked his Texas spirit! I really liked the high-spirited, professional way he piloted the aircraft! I really liked his genuine patriotism, and I especially liked the way he welcomed me as a full-fledged member of our "kick the tires and light the fires" combat crew. On December 23, we destroyed one NVN truck in Steel Tiger and we were shot at only once. That was a good ride to get our crew coordination down again. We made every mission count.

On Christmas Eve, I was not scheduled to fly. Those of us who were not scheduled to fly sat by an open fire at the Nimrod patio and listened to tape recordings of Christmas music and waited for the scheduled flight crews to return. Thankfully, they all returned that night. We greeted each crew with a hearty "Merry Christmas"!!! We also gave them some spirits to match our spirits. I *really* missed Dianne and Kim that night.

Christmas was a day to remember. It was the first Christmas that I had been separated from Dianne and Kimberly. Christmas Eve and

Christmas have always been very special days in my memory. That Christmas was like no other. The day began with me being extremely happy to find two letters from Dianne in my mailbox. In the letters, she told me all about the Christmas preparations and events at home. Later that day, I opened the three presents that Dianne had mailed about a week earlier. I treasured the three presents so much that I almost did not want to open them. However, I got into the Christmas spirit and opened the presents. Dianne sent me some pajamas, handkerchiefs and clothing…all very welcome and needed gifts. Dianne meant the world to me… I loved her and I loved the three wonderful presents she had sent to me.

It was during that unusual Christmas season that I had a most unusual dream. I was asleep in my end of the trailer when I dreamed that I saw a beautiful Christmas scene full of lighted candles and full of thousands of bright white Christmas lights. In the middle of the lighted candles and burning white lights appeared the faces and spirits of Dianne and Kimberly. It was a scene of overwhelming love and joy. I remember it like it was yesterday. Although I didn't know it at the time, it was a foreshadowing of my family and many happy Christmases to follow. Since the time of that dream, I have experienced the same joy each Christmas with Dianne, Kim, Kristi (our second daughter), Ryan (our son), Bill (Kristi's husband), and Colette, Averi, and Chase (our grandchildren). God sometimes allows our most wonderful dreams to become reality. His treasures are the lights in the spirits and souls of our family members.

On Christmas night I flew a combat mission. It seemed so unnatural. It seemed like it never should have happened. It just didn't seem right. But it happened. I remember having a great Christmas dinner at the Officers' Club at NKP; I remember being entertained by a Japanese musical group; and I remember the stark reality of preparing to fly a combat mission on Christmas night, December 25, 1967. We had to mentally switch gears from the nostalgia of Christmas to the reality of war. We donned our flight suits and strapped on our .38 caliber revolvers. We attended the intelligence briefings and we pre-flighted the aircraft. We started the engines and we roared down the runway. It was supposed to be a Christmas truce. That was a joke. The NVN were taking advantage of the so-called Christmas truce to move supplies down the Ho Chi Minh Trail. Our squadron got about 30 NVN supply trucks that night. However, the price we paid was a lost T-28 (Zorro) pilot, two downed helicopters, and a ground TACAN navigation station that was lost due to enemy action. In a religious and spiritual sense, Christmas meant everything to us. Christmas meant nothing to our enemy.

d. Loss of Carlos, Bill and Paul

On the night of December 29, 1967, the unthinkable happened. We lost Captain Carlos Cruz (pilot), Captain Bill Potter (navigator/co-pilot) and Staff Sergeant Paul Foster (scope operator). Carlos and Bill had flown more than 100 combat missions and were recognized by all Nimrods as being the best of the best. Sergeant Paul Foster, only twenty-two years old at the time, volunteered during that mission to occupy the gunner's position in the fuselage of the aircraft, which enabled him to observe the enemy truck traffic along the Ho Chi Minh Trail that night using a Starlight Scope (night-vision scope). Paul could see the trucks using the night-vision Starlight Scope, mark the target, and enable Carlos and Bill to roll-in and attack the target at night. Normally, we did not fly with anyone occupying the gunner's position, but occasionally we would fly with a volunteer Non-Commissioned Officer (NCO) qualified to operate the hand-held Starlight Scope. Paul didn't have to fly on that mission, but like Carlos and Bill, on the night of December 29, 1967, had a rendezvous with destiny. Incredibly, for me personally, it had only been twenty-five days since I flew my first combat familiarization mission with Carlos and Bill. As Pappy and I heard the radio call on the night of December 29, 1967, that the A-26 flown by Carlos, Bill and Paul had been hit by AAA, my first combat familiarization ride on December 4, 1967, seemed like a lifetime ago.

At the time, Carlos was Captain Carlos Cruz, a twenty-nine year old U. S. Air Force pilot originally from Arroyo, Puerto Rico. He was one of the most aggressive and effective combat pilots I had ever met. Bill was Captain William Joseph Potter, Jr., an uncommonly calm and effective navigator/co-pilot from Ambridge, Pennsylvania, thirty-two years of age, and a dedicated professional who had volunteered for a six-month extension of his almost complete one-year combat assignment.

Paul was Staff Sergeant Paul Foster, age twenty-two, night-vision scope operator and a true patriot from Knoxville, Tennessee.

The night before, Pappy and I had flown another horrendous mission. No sooner had we reached the Steel Tiger area of operations than we were directed to orbit over a downed F-4C. The F-4C crew had been shot down with 23-millimeter ZPU antiaircraft fire. Both F-4C pilots had managed to eject successfully just before their aircraft impacted with the ground. I could hear both of them plainly on the ground. They were talking to us with their survival rescue radios. The aircraft commander was all right but the back-seat pilot's chute was hung up in the cliff-like karst, and he had sustained a head injury. Pappy and I orbited over the area for more than two hours while rescue helicopters and "Sandies" (A-1E single engine attack aircraft) attempted to rescue the two F-4C pilots. Despite "all-out" rescue efforts, the operation had to be called off until sunrise because of intense AAA and darkness. Pappy and I were forced to return to NKP. To our great joy, we learned after landing that both F-4C pilots had been rescued. For us, the rescue celebration was short-lived. The very next day brought another mission and the loss of Carlos, Bill and Paul.

I was in shock and denial. My guess is that Pappy felt the same way. On the night of December 29, Pappy and I took off about thirty minutes after Carlos and his crew took off. Pappy and I were only about fifteen miles north of them in Steel Tiger when we heard the radio report that they had been hit by antiaircraft fire. We heard Carlos' radio report stating that they had been hit by AAA fire, that they were just over treetop level, and that they could not get out. Then the radio communications with Carlos and crew went silent. Pappy and I immediately turned and flew to their last known position. I distinctly remember looking down as we approached that position. As we approached, there was a large area of fire and smoke on the ground that appeared to be the crash impact area. We could not establish radio contact. We orbited the area for a long time hoping to establish contact with Carlos, Bill or Paul. It did not happen. We felt so helpless and we were in such pain. Finally, we had no recourse other than to fly to a different location, strike the enemy with our remaining ordnance, and return to base. We subconsciously flew our A-26 aircraft on the return trip home. We were somewhat numb, but the loss made us even

41

more determined to win the war.

e. The "Pro" Missions with Col. Farmer

When I arrived at NKP in November of 1967, the commander of the 609th Air Commando Squadron was Lt. Colonel Howard Farmer. Typically, at that time in Air Force history, the squadron commander was a senior lieutenant colonel, and typically, the rest of us referred to him as Colonel Farmer, or more simply as, the "Colonel." I immediately noticed that Colonel Farmer had the deep respect of every member of the squadron. I heard that Colonel Farmer had become the squadron commander in the summer of 1967 as a result of Lt. Colonel Bruce Jensen (the previous squadron commander) being shot down and killed on his last (or next to last) scheduled combat mission. Other than that, I didn't know much about Colonel Farmer's background, but I can easily describe his appearance and his demeanor. Since I was twenty-five years old when I reported for A-26 duty at NKP, anyone forty years of age or older seemed quite senior. Colonel Farmer must have been in his mid-forties at the time. He was of medium height and he had broad shoulders. His hair was cut short—almost a burr—and he had some gray hair mixed in with the dark brown hair. Several characteristics stood out about his appearance. He was absolutely calm and collected. His large blue eyes penetrated to the core of everybody and everything within his field of view. He had a bright twinkle in his eyes. At the same time, you could tell that he was shouldering a tremendous responsibility, and that he was up to the task. It's no wonder we all had so much respect for Colonel Farmer. He was one of those rare leaders you never forget.

Not only was Colonel Farmer a great leader, he was also a great combat pilot and teacher. He flew with us and taught us by example. My diary brings it all back to life again. On January 20, 1968, my 31st combat mission into Steel Tiger, Colonel Farmer, as the instructor pilot, sat in the right seat for the final combat area checkout ride for Major Mark Richards, one of our new pilots. I sat in the jump seat directly behind Colonel Farmer. Major Richards was in the left seat. Major Richards impressed me as being a flamboyant and likable pilot, and at the same time, a man who had a wife and family he wanted to return to some day. As we approached the target area, Colonel Farmer calmly coached everybody on what needed to be done. We watched a B-57 crew work over four trucks on the Trail, and after the B-57 crew departed the area, we teamed up with the FAC aircraft and continued the strikes against the trucks and gun positions below. What I particularly remember about Col. Farmer in the air had to do with his absolute no-nonsense calm control of the situation, and his unquestioned determination and courage to take on and take out the enemy. It was infectious. The lesson took with Mark and me.

Colonel Farmer did it again the next night with Major Grob and me—almost a repeat of the night before. We flew to the same area. We initially watched another B-57 strike the target. The B-57 crew dropped 750-pound napalm canisters on a truck convoy and had several trucks burning. Alley Cat cleared a reconnaissance F-4C to fly over the area to take aerial photographs. The F-4C crew screamed over the area, dropped photoflash cartridges, took photos, and departed with 37-millimeter tracers racing after the aircraft. By that time we were getting low on fuel, so we took our turn on the target. We made six passes in blistering 37-millimeter fire. We hit trucks and antiaircraft gun positions. Major Grob was one smooth pilot. We did our duty and returned to NKP.

After that flight, the last mission I remember with Colonel Farmer was the final combat area checkout ride with Captain Chuck Kenyon. It was a mission much like the missions described above. If I remember correctly, both Major Grob and Captain Kenyon flew with an A-26 unit in Panama before reporting for duty in Thailand. One distinct scene stands out in my mind concerning the Captain Kenyon checkout ride. As Colonel Farmer coached Captain Kenyon to nose over and attack a truck convoy at the same general location in Steel Tiger, a stream of long, wide, red-colored tracers appeared just in front of the nose of the aircraft. Captain Chuck Kenyon was another "Cool Hand Luke." He simply steepened the dive. I remember seeing the determined glare in his eyes as he pressed the attack. I also remember Colonel Farmer calmly and courageously directing the attacks. The red tracers were huge as they passed just over the canopy. That meant they were very close to striking the aircraft. Chuck was superb. The Colonel was a "Pro." Thanks to Col. Farmer, Chuck and I learned what we needed to know to sharpen our skills and become effective A-26 crewmembers on the Ho Chi Minh Trail.

f. The "Last Bullet" Mission with Robbie

How can I describe Major Edward M. Robinson, the penultimate, seasoned A-26 pilot? We all knew Major Robinson as "Robbie." My recollection is that he was a polite, matter-of-fact person. He was also a lethal fighter pilot. Back at NKP, he was one of the nicest, most polite gentlemen you would ever want to meet. At the controls of the A-26 on any given combat mission, he calmly, and with full dedication to duty, delivered every available flare, rocket, napalm canister, incendiary firebomb, hard bomb, and .50 caliber machine gun bullet directly into the laps of the enemy until all ordnance was expended. Robbie had nerves of steel. I can still see him in his green flight suit. He was probably about forty-five years old, he was a confident and calm man, and he had an expression in his dark eyes that seemed to defy understanding (my impression: Robbie was a human shark). Some members of our squadron thought Robbie had a death wish. I don't know. I do know that I had the rare privilege of joining Robbie on two of those missions, and I was thankful that I survived both adventures.

On February 22, 1968, my 47th combat mission, Robbie and I flew a most unusual mission. We were scheduled to fly north some 200 miles to Barrel Roll, which we did without any Nav Aids (TACAN and VOR were out), but we were later diverted to the Steel Tiger area where we made about twelve dive-bombing passes on trucks. The part that I vividly remember had to do with attacking the enemy after all of the bombs had been delivered on target. What did we have left? Why, we had eight .50 caliber machine guns and full-up ammo in the nose of the aircraft. What made me airsick in A-26 training at England AFB, Louisiana? Yes, that's right, firing the nose guns as you dive and bank and hose targets and climb and fill the cockpit with nauseating smoke. As I glanced left at Robbie, I could tell that he had never been airsick. With those dark, blank eyes that any shark would be proud of, Robbie circled the target area and repeatedly "popped off" high-intensity flares that descended on small parachutes and fully illuminated the Steel Tiger road structure below. According to my diary, we made about twelve passes on a truck convoy, and when all of our bombs were gone, we made about five passes with our .50 caliber machine guns down on the deck. It must have been about five o'clock in the morning, local time. I remember it very clearly. Robbie and I were down on the deck at treetop level, late at night over the Ho Chi Minh Trail in eastern Laos…exhausted but determined… looking for targets. I was so exhausted that I didn't know how much longer I could hang on. Then…we spotted several trucks. Robbie nosed down slightly and pressed the gun triggers. The nose of our aircraft became a flashing, attacking machine. Robbie was in his realm. I wanted to live. I don't know what Robbie wanted. We continued to make repeated strafing attacks down on the deck. Imagine that scene at five o'clock in the morning…you are tired…the whole tree and road area immediately below you is illuminated by high-intensity flares…and you are making repeated strafing attacks on targets at high speed as you maneuver in an out of light, darkness, smoke, and skirt the tops of tropical trees. One minor flight miscalculation and you are going to slam into the trees or the ground. Robbie was totally energized and he was intent on taking out the enemy. He was successful. That night, to the best of my recollection, we fired each and every .50 caliber machine gun bullet (at least 1600 machine gun bullets) from our eight nose machine guns as we made repeated passes above the tropical trees. Robbie chewed up anything and everything in our path. He didn't quit until he had fired the last bullet. We were flying at what seemed like an incredible speed. Treetops were flying by, and smoke was flying by, and we were intent on attacking whatever moved. For whatever reason, at that most unusual time, I had a momentary flashback…to an earlier mission with Major Edward M. Robinson.

On January 27, 1968, I flew a rather hairy mission with Major Robinson. That was Steel Tiger mission No. 36 for me. At the time, the mission seemed rather routine. Looking back, it was extraordinary. Robbie and I were flying in the same target area with three B-57s, three A-26s, an O-1E, a C-130, and an RF-4C reconnaissance bird. As I noted in my diary, that many aircraft, combined with numerous trucks and six to eight persistent antiaircraft gunners, makes for a most interesting situation. I'm surprised that the antiaircraft gunners didn't hit one or more of our aircraft, or that we didn't have a mid-air collision.

I don't know the total number of enemy supply trucks destroyed in the confusion, but I'm sure it was better than twenty. Amazingly enough, all of our aircraft made it home safely. Robbie was the hallmark of an outstanding attack military pilot. None better. That mission earned me a few days off in Bangkok—I needed it!

g. The Lima Site 85 Mission with Col. Learmonth

On the night of March 10, 1968, Lt. Colonel Allen Learmonth and I unknowingly flew a historic mission. I knew that Lt. Colonel Learmonth was a heavyweight as far as officers were concerned at NKP. He was the Vice Commander of the 56th Special Operations Wing, and he was already on the promotion list to be promoted to full Colonel. It was my good fortune to be assigned to fly with him from time to time. He was much like Lt. Col. Farmer and Lt. Col. Shippey—senior combat officers who were true professionals and who had the respect of all of the officers and enlisted personnel at NKP. Colonel Learmonth had some mixed gray hair in his sideburns, he was a calm and collected gentleman (calm blue eyes), he knew how to hit the enemy where it hurts, and he was a true professional A-26 pilot flying combat missions out of NKP.

As we pulled up the gear and flaps, and took up a northwesterly heading toward Barrel Roll on the night of March 10, 1968, Col. Learmonth and I had no idea what was in store for us. We checked in with Alley Cat, acknowledged the assignment that we were to proceed to Lima Site 85, and adjusted the throttles, RPM levers and mixture levers as we climbed to our cruise altitude of 11,000 feet. I can clearly recall the sensation of departing the airfield at NKP, turning northwest toward the Barrel Roll area of operations, and sitting back in the seat at an elevated angle as the engines and props labored to climb out to cruise altitude. Imagine for a moment that you are there with us. The engines and the propellers are roaring with great determination. The instrument panel in front of us is alive with instrument displays, colors and key airspeed, heading and altitude information. As we look out at the wings, the faint light from the moon and stars illuminates the whirring propellers, the wings and the wing-tip fuel tanks. As we reach the cruise altitude of 11,000 feet, we retard the throttles, RPM levers and mixture levers for maximum fuel efficiency. Less than an hour later, we arrive in the vicinity of Lima Site 85. We are poised to attack.

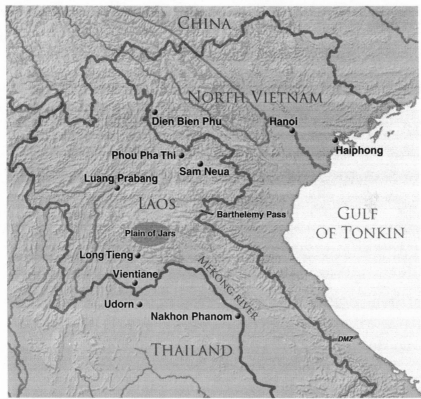

Lima Site 85, perched on the top of Phou Pha Thi, was situated in the part of Laos where the enemy was the strongest. The mountain was 15 miles from the Laos-North Vietnam border and fewer than 30 miles from Sam Neua, the capital of the Pathet Lao. (Staff map by Zaur Eylanbekov) (Reprinted by permission from Air Force Magazine, published by the Air Force Association)

Once at Lima Site 85, all hell broke loose. Lima Site 85 was a very important site in northern Laos. Not only was it a TACAN navigational site, it was also a classified radar site for bombing targets in North Vietnam. Lima Site 85 was literally located on the top of a remote mountain called Phou Pha Thi. A picture is worth a thousand words. The aerial photograph of Lima Site 85 in northern Laos is an incredible photograph.

Three sides of Phou Pha Thi were nearly vertical; the fourth was heavily fortified. Lima Site 85 perched on the very top of the bluff. Imagine U.S. military personnel under attack at night at such a site; imagine U.S. aircrews conducting close air support missions at such a site at night in bad weather. (Joint Task Force-Full Accounting photo) (Reprinted by permission from the Joint Task Force)

How could such sophisticated radar bombing and navigational aids have been constructed on that remote mountaintop in 1967-68? Only our top-level political and military leaders know. As a navigator-bombardier, I knew that Lima Site 85 was a key navigational aid, and I also knew that the classified bombing radar site meant that Hanoi was only 160 miles from the site and vulnerable to precision radar attack around the clock and in all types of weather. Col. Learmonth and I found out on the night of March 10th that the communists also understood the importance of Lima Site 85.

As Col. Learmonth and I flew into the vicinity of Lima Site 85 that night, we saw an impressive display of enemy firepower. The NVN and Pathet Lao forces were mounting a full-scale attack on Lima Site 85. We observed a multitude of muzzle flashes, tracers, and incendiary trajectories indicating that enemy troops were firing small arms fire and mortars and small rockets into the friendly forces at Lima Site 85. The weather was terrible. Thunderstorms and lightning were everywhere. We were in and out of rain and lightning. I remember being tossed about in the cockpit. In that cauldron of light and shadows, we communicated as best we could with our fellow American fighting men below. We made repeated dive-bombing attacks on the enemy units that were firing at Lima Site 85, unloading all of our ordnance directly into the midst of the enemy troops below. At the end of our attacks that night, the enemy troops simply stopped shooting. Unfortunately, that is not the end of the story.

According to my diary, we learned the following day that the enemy troops overran Lima Site 85 just before sunup and killed at least eleven Americans—helicopters managed to rescue several men from the site. Unofficial records state that this was the largest single ground combat loss of USAF personnel during the Vietnam War. Colonel Learmonth and I were stunned to hear the bad news, and NKP went into mourning. (For an outstanding article that tells the incredible full story of the fall of Lima Site 85, see Correll, John. T., "The Fall of Lima Site 85," **Air Force Magazine**, April 2006, p. 66.)

h. The Longest Barrel Roll Mission

The longest combat mission I recorded in my diary was a five hour and twenty minute nighttime mission into the Barrel Roll area of operations on April 19, 1968. Actually, another Barrel Roll combat mission of four hours and forty-five minutes on February 17 qualifies as the longest mission with only one landing. First, I will describe the April 19 mission.

On April 19, 1968, I flew with Major Bobby Joe Sears, and Major Douglas (Doug) Carmichael, a newly arrived pilot who was flying one of his initial checkout rides. We flew to northern Laos to Lima Site 59 and made twelve bombing and strafing passes in support of Hmong and Royal Laotian forces. After arriving back in the NKP area we learned that a B-57 was blocking the runway with two blown tires. We were too short on fuel to wait for the field to reopen so we flew over to Udorn RTAFB where we landed, refueled, and took off again for the return flight back to NKP. We finally landed at NKP at five o'clock in the morning. We had experienced a real workout. "Pappy" Sears was his usual self—get the job done no matter what it takes. "Doug" Carmichael, a sharp, likable man beginning to show a hint of gray in his sideburns, impressed me as being a mature officer and a gifted pilot. He was a welcome addition to the squadron. This was my 75th mission.

I was just happy to get back to NKP after a long night from hell.

But let me get back to the other contender for my longest mission in the Vietnam War. On February 17, 1968, I flew a four hour and forty-five minute memorable mission into Barrel Roll with Lt. Colonel John J. Shippey (pilot) and Airman Huffman (Starlight Scope operator). That day happened to be another black day for the Navy squadron assigned at Nakhon Phanom RTAFB. One of their aircraft—a P-2V— was shot down during daylight hours in the same area in Steel Tiger that Major Sears and I had flown into the night before. There were nine crewmembers aboard the U.S. Navy P-2V, and it appeared that all nine had been killed in action.

Knowing that the Navy P-2V and its crew were down, Lt. Colonel John Shippey (pilot), myself (navigator/co-pilot), and Airman Huffman (Starlight Scope operator) took off for another memorable Barrel Roll mission. We flew for four hours and forty-five minutes. Horrendous, bad stormy weather covered most of the area of our flight. At one point, I vividly recall Col. Shippey talking on the intercom about the fact that we were flying over Dien Bien Phu, North Vietnam, the site of the French defeat in 1954. As a navigator, I was alert to the fact that we were flying relatively close to the border of China, and naturally I wanted to keep our aircraft south of China. Our best navigation aid in the area, a TACAN station in northeast Laos near the North Vietnam border, kept us out of trouble. I remember looking down at the nighttime terrain below, as we flew directly over Dien Bien Phu. Just flying over that location made me nervous. I wondered if we were flying too close to China. We finally struck a pre-briefed target before returning to NKP. In my diary, I noted that we saw an unusually bright shooting star that night as we returned to base. It was huge and streaked across the entire sky. I had never seen such a magnificent shooting star before. By the same token, until that night, I had never flown over Dien Bien Phu before, or flown that close to the Chinese border.

i. The Shortest Steel Tiger Mission

My shortest Steel Tiger mission was flown with Major Kenneth (Ken) Yancey. In my diary, I noted that I had flown a "quickie" mission with Yancey. We flew some thirty miles east of NKP and were directed by a FAC aircraft to strike a target east of Takhet, Laos. I thought it was very unusual to be striking a target that close to the Mekong River and the Thai border. We never knew how close the enemy was operating in the NKP area. Since NKP was located adjacent to the Mekong River and the border with Laos, we knew that the Pathet Lao and North Vietnamese communists were operating near or around NKP. As a matter of fact, the security guards at NKP had experienced several battles with suspected insurgents trying to overcome the defenses at NKP. I recall a time period when we watched friendly air strikes on enemy forces just across the Mekong River in Laos. I felt good that Yancey and I had put in several air strikes into enemy forces across the Mekong River. As an aside, our aircraft wanted to roll to the left during high-speed dives and pull-ups. We didn't like that experience. However, we corrected for those unexpected flight characteristics and configured the aircraft for the return flight to NKP. I made the landing…not too bad.

j. Loss of "Bo" Hertlein—Spirit of the Nimrods

This is one of the most painful points in this story. I need to try to tell you about the loss of Captain George B. Hertlein III. His middle name was Bernhard, but for a long time, I thought it was Beauregard. He was from Decatur, Georgia. In my recollection, he was the spirit of the Nimrods. We all called him "Bo" (I thought of him as "Beau" at the time but later learned that it was "Bo"). In any event, he was "Beau" in my mind and "Bo" was bigger than life. In the Civil War era, Bo would have been a fearless horse cavalry officer leading a charge directly into the face of the enemy.

How can you go on if you lose your spirit? Upon reflection, we certainly did lose Bo in combat on the night of April 24, 1968, but I believe we were able to go on because we didn't really lose his indomitable spirit. His fighting spirit never left us.

I need to reflect back now, to think back, and to focus on my first meeting with George B. Hertlein III. We first met during A-26 combat crew training in 1967 at England AFB, Alexandria, Louisiana. My first impression was that Bo was a very likeable person. He loved to fly. He loved to laugh. He had a wonderful Southern accent. He was full of life and we loved him. I don't know how it happened, but during A-26 training at England AFB, Bo and Lt. Colonel John Shippey became a crew. My next recollection concerning Bo is that he and Major Bobby Sears ferried an A-26 aircraft to NKP, Thailand after combat crew training in Louisiana. An A-26 ferry flight from the United States to Thailand was a major accomplishment in itself. But those early impressions didn't begin to do Bo justice.

My next memory of Bo took place after I arrived at NKP, Thailand in November of 1967. It is difficult to describe, but I would like to try to describe the scene to you. In November of 1967, I had just arrived at NKP after the pain of leaving Dianne and Kimberly back in West Virginia. I was definitely suffering from culture shock as I arrived at NKP and renewed friendships with fellow crewmembers. I ran into Bo soon after arrival at NKP. I recall looking directly into Bo's bright blue eyes. Bo was wearing a dark green "many times washed" USAF flight suit with dark black rank insignia. Bo stood about five feet ten inches tall, he was sporting a huge Southeast Asia "curled" mustache, and he was beginning to suffer from a thinning hairline. Bo was smiling, he had a huge contagious twinkle in his eyes, and right in front of me, he lifted his arms and hands to tweak his mustache. Can you see him??? I can still see him. Bo impressed me as being a warrior from the ages. I can attest that Bo had a spirit of the ages. Bo's spirit, whether it was from the ages, or from the South, represented the true fighting spirit of the Nimrods.

I recall many times being airborne on a mission and hearing Bo and Col. Shippey report in to Alley Cat, the C-130 Airborne Combat Control Center, as we flew various missions. Bo frequently handled radio communications for their crew. His voice was always loud and clear—and there was no mistaking his Southern accent. He always made you feel like the U.S.A. flag had just been unfurled and that he and Col. Shippey were ready to lead yet another charge directly into the face of the enemy. His voice inspired you to gather your courage for yet another night of combat. Bo's spirit was…and simply is… unforgettable.

On April 24, 1968, Bo was killed in combat. My diary says that Lt. Colonel Shippey and Bo's aircraft was hit with five or six rounds from an antiaircraft gun. They were hit as they made a dive-bombing pass on a target. According to my diary, Bo was struck in his right shoulder. **My recollection is that Col. Shippey came back and told us that Bo had been hit and was lost in combat. We were numb with denial!** Colonel Shippey had a shocked expression in his eyes. John Shippey was one of our very best…and he had just lived through the nightmare of losing Bo, his good friend and fellow crewmember. It's a real tribute to Col. Shippey that he was able to regain control of the aircraft and make it back to NKP for a landing despite the horror of Bo bleeding to death right beside him in the aircraft, and despite the damage to the aircraft.

I did not immediately visit the aircraft containing Bo's body, but I heard a lot of people talk about the antiaircraft bullet hole in the front of the canopy of the aircraft. Some time later, I visited the aircraft to see for myself. There was, in fact, a hole in the right side of the canopy directly in front of where Bo was sitting on the night of that fateful mission. As Col. John Shippey and Capt. Bo Hertlein bravely and aggressively made yet another nighttime dive-bombing attack on the enemy below, the horrible event actually occurred. We all knew that this same result could happen to any given crew on any given night. We had seen too many tracers race by the canopy as we dived into yet another target area. Even if the enemy didn't have radar-guided antiaircraft guns to hit us at night, they had an ever-increasing huge inventory of Russian and Chinese World War II era antiaircraft guns on the Trail to throw up huge barrages of antiaircraft fire as we attacked the targets. The enemy gunners could hear the different sounds our aircraft made as we nosed over into a dive to attack targets. They responded by throwing up a huge barrage of antiaircraft fire over the target area. Somehow, on the night of April 24, 1968, the bullets from one of those antiaircraft guns ripped through Col. Shippey and Bo's aircraft as they pressed the attack.

On April 26, the entire squadron attended a memorial service for Bo at the base chapel. Chaplain (Major) Cole presided at the service. The cover of the Memorial Service program showed a picture of the cracked U.S. Liberty Bell, flanked on each side by a United States flag, and above the Liberty Bell appeared a quote by Richard Powell: "Freedom is a light for which many men have died in darkness." The service was brief but it was a dignified and impressive tribute to Bo. We will never forget him.

How can you kill the spirit of the Nimrods? How can you kill George B. Hertlein III? The truth is that you can kill an individual (at least as far as our time on Earth is concerned), even a key individual like "Bo," but you can never kill the spirit of a true combat organization unless you kill everyone in the organization. That's what happened in the Vietnam War, we lost key individuals, but we continued to fight. We discovered a strength that we didn't know we had. As it turned out, Bo's spirit had not been killed at all. His spirit stayed with us and made us a far stronger and better combat organization.

k. The "Pro" Mission with Col. Shippey

According to my diary, I had the honor of flying with Lt. Colonel John Shippey on his next combat mission after the shocking mission when Bo was killed in action. The mission took place on the night of April 28, 1968, and we flew for two hours and thirty minutes in the Steel Tiger area of operations. I noted in my diary that Col. Shippey was surprisingly calm and effective considering that Bo's death was still fresh on his mind. I can only imagine what was really going on in his mind during the mission. We made repeated dive-bombing attacks along a heavily defended section of the Trail. The trucks were moving and the AAA was blistering. Col. Shippey was just as aggressive as ever, and he was just as smart as ever. He had the guts to take the fight to the enemy, and the intellect to avoid foolish mistakes. Colonel Shippey was a natural pilot and a natural leader. In short, Col. Shippey was the true combat professional. It was a joy to fly with him. I felt like we were part of a well-oiled machine as we delivered ordnance on the target, pulled up to assess the next bomb run, and coordinated our attacks with the FAC and each other. After we had expended all our ordnance, the FAC aircraft pilot flew near the target area and gave us credit for destroying three trucks, silencing one 37-millimeter gun position, and causing five large secondary fires and numerous secondary explosions.

Something else stands out in my mind about that mission with Col. Shippey. After we landed, I recall taxiing to the far southern end of the runway and stopping the aircraft shortly after we pulled off the active runway. My recollection is that we suspected that one or more of our eight .50 caliber machine guns in the nose of the aircraft might have jammed during the mission, and we wanted the ordnance crew to check the guns and render them safe before we taxied to the parking area. I recall that we shut down the engines, opened the two canopy sections above our seats, and stood up on the seats to get some fresh air as the guns were being checked. That's when a very memorable thing happened. Col. Shippey turned to me in the semi-darkness, looked directly into my eyes, and asked, "Do I scare you?" For whatever reason, I immediately replied, "Not if you will listen to me." His expression didn't change. We didn't try to elaborate. If I had it to do over again I would try to say something better. Col. Shippey was the ultimate "pro." I certainly didn't mean that I wanted to try to tell him how to pilot the airplane or attack the enemy. He was an absolute expert pilot at flying the airplane. What I was really trying to say was that we are partners in this very dangerous operation, and I want to be aggressive and smart with you. I only ask that you listen to me for my contribution as we risk our lives in combat. I can still see Col. Shippey's face and eyes during that brief exchange. I believe he understood what I was trying to say. I also believe that he would never have asked the question if he had not experienced the trauma of losing Bo on the previous mission.

Colonel Shippey was one of our inspirational leaders the entire time I was at NKP. I didn't find out until much later, but John Shippey was also a veteran of the Korean War. Unknown to me at the time, he had flown many B-26 combat missions as a younger pilot during the Korean War. This was his second war. How many people have the courage to face up to their first war, much less their second war? Col. John Shippey represents the ideal true U.S. Air Force leader and combat professional. Later, in the summer of 1968, he became our squadron commander. A better choice could not have been made. He had the respect and admiration of every member of the squadron. He was always calm, collected, fearless, and he fought to win. He was an expert pilot and he took a genuine interest in every member of the squadron. He was serious about getting the job done, but at the same time he had a twinkle in his eyes and he had a good sense of humor. He was a pro's pro. I loved flying with him.

l.   Loss of Bob and Lou

As I noted in my diary, April 30, 1968, was another "black" day for the Nimrods. On the night of April 30, we lost Captain Robert Pietsch (pilot) and Captain Louis Guillerman (navigator/co-pilot). This was a stunning loss for the entire squadron. It had only been six days since we lost "Bo" Hertlein. Bob and Lou were seasoned combat crewmembers, and they were tremendous individuals. Bob was from Cleveland, Ohio, and Lou was from Westchester, Pennsylvania. Bob was the strong and silent type who was always thinking, and Lou was the talkative, extrovert type who was always engaged and who always had a big smile. After being at NKP for seven months, Bob and Lou had just returned from their Rest & Recuperation (R&R) trip to Hawaii. I understand that Bob was married and had five children. I was not sure about Lou's family situation.

The facts concerning the loss of Bob and Lou were never clear. According to the notes in my diary, we believe that Bob and Lou crashed while striking a target in Steel Tiger. Pappy and I did not fly on the night of April 30, so I had no first-hand information concerning the loss of Bob and Lou. The only thing we knew for certain was that Bob and Lou never returned to NKP following their departure for a combat mission on the night of April 30, 1968. The dry season was about to come to an end during the last of April and the enemy forces were moving as many trucks as possible down the Trail before the rains came and the Ho Chi Minh Trail road network became impassible. It was a time of intense combat. Since Bob and Lou did not return from their mission on April 30, they were officially listed as Missing in Action. The Nimrods were in mourning.

On June 25, 1968, a Service of Prayer and Remembrance was held for Bob and Lou at the NKP base chapel. I remember attending a very dignified service. The cover page of the Chapel Program contained a Bible quote stating, "If we live by the Spirit, let us also walk by the Spirit." Bob and Lou's spirit continued to sustain the Nimrods.

m. The B-52 "Bombs From Above" Mission

On May 18, 1968, Major Sears and I flew a most unusual mission.

This was Mission No. 93 for me. The pre-flight and climb-out were normal as we flew into the Steel Tiger area. Nothing was normal after we leveled off and checked in with Alley Cat. Several things stand out in my memory about that particular mission. First of all, we took off well after midnight. For some unexplained reason, the whole road structure in the Steel Tiger area of operations seemed absolutely dead. There was very little radio chatter, there were no urgent calls to proceed to a target area, there were no visible tracers in the sky, and there were no flashes from bomb detonations on the ground. Pappy must have been as perplexed as I was—we couldn't stir up any trouble, although we tried. We simply maintained radio contact with Alley Cat and continued patrolling up and down the Ho Chi Minh Trail in a north to south direction. As a matter of fact, the action was so slow that we eventually found ourselves all the way down south to Saravanne (sometimes spelled Saravan). We knew our location because there was a TACAN navigation aid located at Saravanne. We almost never flew that far south. We were not too many miles north of the Cambodia border. I remember it being in the very wee hours of the morning. It was very dark and very lonely. I was tired, Pappy was tired, and we were not finding any targets despite popping numerous high-intensity flares over the dirt roads below. We strained our eyes in the darkness to see anything that might be a target. All we could see were vacant roads, darkness below and stars above, and endless treetops. Exhaustion was setting in and it's fair to say we were getting very tired and very bored.

And then it happened. All of a sudden all hell broke loose!!! The ground below us simply erupted into a cauldron of churning explosions and mind-bending, high-intensity flashes of light. I don't know about Pappy, but I damn near went into cardiac arrest! Pappy didn't miss a beat. He immediately applied power and banked hard left to turn away from the unexpected threat. It's an understatement to say that we were in shock. We quickly returned to level flight and continued to watch the ground erupt in a long, continuous string of explosions and blinding flashes of light. As a former B-52 navigator-bombardier, I quickly understood what was happening. A B-52 bomb release from high altitude was impacting and detonating in the immediate road structure we were flying over. Too bad we didn't get the word about the planned B-52 bomb drop. But then, I am a realist. In war, you can't always expect to be briefed on all scheduled combat missions in your area of operations. We were most fortunate that none of the bombs from the unexpected B-52 bomb drop struck our aircraft. It was a close call. We were most thankful to make it back to NKP after that terrifying experience.

n. A Typical Dry Season Steel Tiger Mission with "Pappy" Sears

Would you like to strap on a vintage World War II A-26 dive-bomber in the Vietnam War and experience a combat mission? All right, this is what it was like. You do not sleep well and you fret and fume until you approach the aircraft. It's nighttime and your anxiety begins to fade away as you go to work.

You approach the two-engine propeller aircraft from the right side and you pull down the ascent ladder. Before you climb into the cockpit, you do a walk-around. You concentrate on the flying control surfaces, and even more, on the ordnance that has been loaded for the mission. You walk around and you see a bomb load that dates back from World War II. From the eight wing pylon stations, you inspect the typical bomb load of incendiary bombs, napalm, rockets, CBU canisters, high-incendiary flares and hard bombs. The bomb bay load typically includes numerous hard bombs (e.g., finned 500 to 750-pound gravity-fall bombs), and the nose gun section typically includes a full load of ammunition for the eight .50 caliber machine guns. You inspect the control surfaces, focusing on the flaps, the ailerons, and the elevators. You inspect the copper wires leading to the fuses on the bombs. You inspect the .50 caliber machine guns and their chambers in the aircraft nose section. You walk on top of the wings and check out the top of the aircraft. You inspect the gray paint that the armament crew has just applied to the bombs, rockets, flare dispensers and CBU canisters, and you inwardly shout, we are good to go!!! You know that your life depends on the incredibly hard work and skill of the maintenance and armament personnel, and you take every opportunity to thank them and let them know they are genuinely appreciated.

Time for another take-off! The engines have just been checked during the pre-flight run-up. We receive clearance for take-off, and we release the brakes and roll onto the active runway. It is early nighttime.

My great friend and pilot, Major Bobby J. Sears ("Pappy") of Texas, has just pushed the throttles full forward, and my job as the navigator/co-pilot is to monitor the instruments, push the RPM and Mixture levers to full forward, and hold all the levers full forward with my left hand as we race down the runway and leap into the air. This is not an easy task with a full bomb load. You could die on any given take-off. Anyway, we make it seem like a routine take-off run. The two Pratt & Whitney R-2800 engines are roaring on the take-off roll, the propellers are biting every ounce of air, and at a speed of approximately 135 mph, the A-26 Invader lifts off the Nakhon Phanom RTAFB runway. I vividly remember being there. The aircraft strains and groans and we are airborne! We retract the gear and the flaps and we steer the aircraft straight ahead. I monitor the instrument panel and hear the laboring of the engines as we climb to our attack altitude. We turn toward the east as our A-26 Invader climbs into the darkness of yet another mission. This is war and we are the warriors—we have been trained and we are ready. The pre-flight apprehension falls away. Our teamwork kicks in, and we are once again doing our job. We are one with the machine. There is no way to describe the overpowering sound of the engines as they propel us forward. We level off at the altitude assigned by Alley Cat, the C-130 aircraft controlling the combat airspace over our zone of operations in Laos and Vietnam. As we penetrate the darkness and retard the throttles to cruising speed, we quickly adjust the RPM and mixture levers for fuel-efficient and smooth engine operation. The engines then begin the familiar harmonized drone that ensures us all is well. I wish that I could accurately describe the sound of the engines and the propellers as we take-off, climb-out and transition into level flight.

At take-off, the engines and propellers are raising hell and giving us everything they were designed to deliver. During climb-out, the engines and propellers are continuing to perform at maximum military performance as we retract the landing gear and flaps. As we level off at cruise altitude, a magical transformation takes place. We typically level off at anywhere from 7,000 to 11,000 feet altitude, and wait for our assignment. We retard the throttles, RPM levers, and mixture levers. The aircraft roars a powerful but synchronized roar. I will try to describe that incredible harmonic sound to you. All Nimrods would recognize the sound immediately. We have leveled off and almost automatically retard the throttles, RPM levers and mixture levels to cruising speed. The engines and propellers then settle into a familiar and indescribably beautiful harmonic sound. The sound starts as a low, powerful, throaty roar, then transitions to a medium upscale transcending whirring sound, and then smoothly settles into a soothing, hypnotic and repetitive roar. At this point the airframe is riding on a wave of air, the engines and propellers are performing at maximum efficiency, and Pappy and I were hearing a wonderful, repetitive and powerful harmonic sound…roarrr rrrrrrrrrrrrrrrrrrrr…whirrrrrrrrrrrrrrrrrrrrrrr…roarrrrrrrrrrrrrrrrrrrrrrrr…. The aeronautical engineers did their job. We are poised to attack.

We check in with Alley Cat, and we are immediately directed to contact and work with the pilot of a forward air controller aircraft operating in a hot section of Steel Tiger. The date is May 26, 1968, and it is my 102nd combat mission. We primarily navigate using a TACAN radio navigational aid and we have the frequency of NKP dialed into this basic but very reliable navigation aid that gives us a bearing and distance to that TACAN station. Using TACAN, we know our present position, enabling us to immediately change our heading to fly directly to Nail 22, the forward air controller aircraft. We change our communication radio to the Nail 22 frequency and let him know that Nimrod 26 is en route. We can see all hell breaking loose as we approach Delta 57, one of the hotbed locations on the Ho Chi Minh Trail at night. Tracers are filling the sky from multiple directions. Bombs are detonating along the Trail as we approach. The radio chatter lets us know that another Nimrod crew and a B-57 Red Bird crew are engaged in making strikes in a heavily defended area of the road network below. As we approach, Nail 22 efficiently works us into the strike pattern. We are given a bearing and distance to strike from a log (bright incendiary object on the ground dropped by Nail 22) and I turn on the Master Bomb Control Switch and ask Pappy what ordnance he wants to use on the first pass. He elects to use the two incendiary bombs and I select wing stations 4 and 5. Pappy maneuvers into position, and at the right moment we retard throttles, adjust the RPM levers to place the two engines 100 revolutions per minute apart (creates a great beating sound and confuses enemy gunners on your exact location), and Pappy smoothly pushes the nose of the aircraft over into a dive until he can bring the target into view using the bomb sight mounted on the instrument panel directly in front of him. He has previously dialed in the correct settings for incendiary bombs. As the dive steepens, I call off descending altitudes in 500-foot increments. The two bombs are released, the plane feels lighter, and we apply power and turn sharply to avoid tracers coming up straight ahead. As we climb out from the target area, we turn our heads and witness the bombs detonating on the enemy below.

We begin working a strike pattern where a lead strike aircraft makes a pass at trucks on the road and another strike aircraft rolls in to strike gun positions that are firing at the lead aircraft. Because of bends in the road, bends in the nearby river, and being able to see antiaircraft fire initiate from a particular point on the ground, we know when we are successful in knocking out a gun position. We know when we destroy a truck because it usually burns on the road. We alternate with the other two strike aircraft in putting in pass after pass. After dropping all of the ordnance off our eight wing stations, we open the bomb bay doors and push the nose over in another steep dive to drop bombs from the bomb bay. All of a sudden, I am shocked to see an O-2 FAC aircraft flying directly through the airspace we are diving through. Fortunately, Pappy sees him in the same split second, jumps hard on the control yoke and rudder pedals, and we narrowly avoid a mid-air collision with the aircraft that has been expertly directing the action. I close the bomb bay doors. Although we each operate from different assigned altitudes, there is no guarantee that you will always avoid a mid-air situation in the thick of hitting a target with multiple aircraft at night. After we climb back to our assigned altitude, collect our wits about us, ensure that the FAC aircraft is holding in a particular quadrant away from the target area, we once again open the bomb bay doors and release the remainder of our bombs on the last designated target of the night for us.

We say goodnight to the FAC and the two other strike aircraft and check in with Alley Cat to let the Command Post know we are returning to base. We take up a westerly heading toward NKP, I switch to the main fuselage fuel tank and I let Pappy know I am going to light up a cigarette. Pappy doesn't smoke, but he knows that a cigarette helps calm my nerves. We monitor the Alley Cat frequency as we drone toward the Mekong River and NKP. Like too many nights, the radio chatter lets us know that another American aircrew is in trouble. An F-4C crew operating north of the DMZ has taken a major antiaircraft hit and the crew is trying to hang on until they can get the aircraft over Laos or Thailand. A short time later, we hear a report that the two-man crew has bailed out somewhere over Laos. We also hear that NKP rescue choppers are en route to their location. Pappy decides that he wants me to make the landing approach and landing. Pappy, like most of the A-26 pilots, wants his right-seater to be able to land the aircraft in the event the pilot might take a hit in combat and be rendered incapable of flying the aircraft. He takes over radio communications with NKP Approach Control. Since this is my 102nd mission, I comfortably follow heading and altitude directions and turn the aircraft left and line up with the runway on final approach. Pappy and I coordinate to lower the gear, retard the throttles, extend the flaps, and turn on the landing lights. The aircraft touches down and I pull the throttles all the way back. Pappy was almost as pleased with the landing as I was—we coasted to taxi speed and Pappy took over to taxi back to the parking area.

And so ended another fairly routine dry season A-26 combat mission into and out of Steel Tiger. We flew for two hours and twenty minutes. The FAC credited Pappy and me with destroying ten trucks that night. The trucks were loaded with war supplies heading south to re-supply North Vietnam and Viet Cong communist forces operating in South Vietnam. There were some eight antiaircraft guns shooting at us that night in the target area. Pappy and I were awarded Distinguished Flying Crosses for that mission. There was one final item of great news—as we were returning to base, the NKP chopper crew was successful in locating and picking up both crewmembers of the F-4C that was lost due to being hit with antiaircraft fire north of the DMZ. As recorded in my diary, we lost U.S. aircraft and crews almost every day. The rescue chopper crews saved the day for many downed airmen.

o. The "False Start" Abort Mission with Pappy

I had to leaf through my diary for some time to find a reference to this most unusual night at NKP. I finally found it. The night was June 12, 1968, and Pappy and I completed all of the normal procedures leading up to yet another scheduled combat mission. This was going to be Mission No. 107 for me. What I recall so vividly was being in the aircraft cockpit with Pappy prior to take-off. It was nighttime and we had just completed the routine pre-flight engine run-up checks. I was intent on checking and crosschecking all of the lighted flight instruments on the instrument panel and was satisfied that all instrument readings were within normal limits. I recall that Pappy obtained radio clearance for take-off and he advanced the throttles to taxi onto the active runway for the take-off. Everything seemed normal. The aircraft lurched to life and we picked up groundspeed and we initiated a left turn to roll onto the active runway. All of a sudden, and without any kind of warning, the aircraft abruptly fell to the left. We were startled to hear an incomprehensible screaming, high-impact noise, and at the same time, a giant shower of sparks flew in front of us from the left side of the aircraft to the right side of the aircraft. We didn't know what we were dealing with but we instinctively and instantaneously reacted to the situation. We "killed" the engines faster than you can verbalize "emergency," turned off every aircraft switch and control within reach, grabbed the overhead canopy release levers on both sides, threw the canopy sections open above our heads, popped open every seat release and parachute release control lever in our way, practically jumped out of the cockpit and scrambled down the ladder, and raced away from that wild and crazy aircraft that seemed to be trying to kill us!

As I reflect back, I don't understand how we survived that experience. We were fully loaded with fuel, and we were fully loaded with ordnance. In fact, I remember that we were loaded with several large napalm canisters on the wing stations that night. The huge shower of sparks was flying into and over napalm canisters. Why didn't the napalm and other wing ordnance ignite and explode? I don't know. What I do know is that Pappy wasn't through for the night. After the fire trucks and emergency crews responded to the scene, Pappy decided we should immediately find another aircraft. I told you he was from Texas. I believe most crews would have called it a night. We found another A-26, we performed another pre-flight, we roared down the runway, we pulled up the landing gear, and by the grace of God, we flew and survived another combat mission. That hair-raiser lasted three hours and twenty-five minutes. For many reasons, we were very lucky to still be alive.

The next day we learned that the entire left main gear (tire and wheel assembly) had sheared off as we made the left turn onto the active runway. Although we had no way of understanding it at the time, the left main strut impacted the runway after the wheel assembly fell away, resulting in the left engine propeller digging into the runway and causing the giant shower of sparks as the aircraft tilted left and lurched forward minus the left main wheel assembly. That type of unexpected mechanical failure is how combat crewmembers sometimes die. It was not our time. We survived and we flew another mission…aboard another A-26.

p. The Surprise Plain of Jars Mission with Pappy

The Plain of Jars combat activity increased significantly in 1968, especially after President Lyndon Johnson declared a temporary bombing halt over North Vietnam. Although located in northern Laos and considered a part of the Barrel Roll area of operations, the Plain of Jars itself was a huge 500 square-mile, diamond shaped region covered with rolling hills and grassy flatlands, surrounded on all sides by rugged mountains reaching up to 9000 feet and more in elevation. Our A-26 dive-bombing operations were very effective in supporting the courageous Hmong mountain fighters led by Maj. Gen. Vang Pao, and the Royal Laotian forces, against the regular North Vietnamese army units and the local Pathet Lao communist units. We typically flew northwest out of NKP to a crossroads at Phonsavan (Xiang Khoang) and operated as far east as Sam Nua (Xam Nua) and as far north as the northern Laos region just west of Dien Bien Phu. The Plain of Jars got its name from hundreds of huge stone "jars" found in the region that were probably used as burial urns by prehistoric tribes. On one occasion, General Vang Pao invited Nimrod crewmembers that were not scheduled to fly to a meeting in Laos. He said Nimrod crews had saved their lives many times and he showed his appreciation by giving each Nimrod a musket rifle (which they still used) and two rings (a gold one and a silver one). I was flying a combat mission during that meeting so I regrettably did not get to meet General Vang Pao and the Hmong mountain fighters.

One mission particularly stands out in my memory concerning Barrel Roll and Plain of Jars operations. The date was July 1, 1968. After a typical pre-flight, I remember taking off and turning northwest toward the Plain of Jars. Pappy was sitting in the left seat and we were shifting in our seats to make ourselves as comfortable as possible in our parachutes, seat harnesses and helmets as we coordinated communications with NKP departure control and Alley Cat, and made certain that our power settings and heading were correct for the mission in front of us. I recall scanning the instrument panel to make certain the engines were operating within normal limits, and I recall looking out at the wing-tip fuel tanks. I also recall taking a look at Pappy in his fighting gear and fighting persona (all business and set chin) as our propellers bit into the air to gain altitude as we headed north for another unknown mission with the enemy. The engines roared that determined sound that gave us confidence to continue our climb out to 11,000 feet, the altitude we wanted on that Barrel Roll mission to ensure that we were well above the 9500 ft. peaks on our flight path. Unfortunately, we had lost one of our primary TACAN stations in northern Laos to enemy forces in March, so I had to pay very close attention to navigation to make certain we would arrive at the correct destination on that mission.

The climb-out to 11,000 feet deserves more elaboration. Picture yourself in the cockpit of the A-26 turning northwest and climbing out of NKP. The two Pratt & Whitney R-2800 engines are roaring and the propellers are biting the air and you sense that you are part of a flying machine that is gradually gaining altitude. It is nighttime and you are confronted by a maze of lighted flight instruments in front of you. You communicate by radio with NKP departure control and Alley Cat, and you monitor and adjust the flight controls. You pay close attention to navigation and make certain you are on the correct heading. But most of all, you listen to the droning sound of those engines. They are overwhelmingly powerful and they are your lifelines. As you climb with your partner, you mentally prepare for the mission ahead. The roar of the engines is both comforting and overwhelming. As you reach 11,000 feet, after a long climb, the pilot noses the aircraft over to level flight and the two of you pull back the throttles, RPM levers and mixture levers to cruise configurations. The engines seem to instantly respond with great relief, and a new sound sets in as you adjust to cruise altitude. As you "lean the engines" the engines and propellers transition into a sweet, harmonic sound that is impossible to accurately describe, but absolutely amazing to experience.

The mission that night involved establishing communications with one of the Hmong ground FACs. As we approached the Plain of Jars, I recall switching to the VHF frequency for Water Boy, a pre-briefed Hmong ground controller, and keying the mike. "Water Boy," "Water Boy,"…"this is Nimrod 26, how do you read?" "I read you loud and clear, over." "Do you have a target?" "Roger, I hear you, pop a flare." "Roger, popping a flare, do you see it?" "Roger, fly one click ("kilometer") southeast of your flare and pop another flare." "Roger, we are on our way and we just popped another flare." "Do you see our second flare, Water Boy?" "Roger, Roger, put in a strike immediately below your second flare!!!" "Roger, we just dropped a bomb, do you see it?" "Roger, Roger, I see it and you hit the target! Please hit the same target with every thing that you have!!!" "Roger, we are illuminating the area with flares and we are hitting the area with all of our ordnance." I recall seeing the incredibly mountainous terrain below the flares as we turned, banked, dived and climbed. We made pass after pass on the target area until we had expended all ordnance except for what .50 caliber machine gun rounds we might have had left. Water Boy was beside himself on the radio! We had done the job we were trained to do. Judging from Water Boy's excited reaction, we must have plastered the NVN and Pathet Lao that night. I recall feeling good about helping Gen. Vang Pao's Hmong mountain fighters that night as we climbed to recovery altitude and prepared to head southeast to NKP. I thought the mission was over. Not true!

As we leveled off and prepared to fly back to NKP, we established radio contact with two other A-26 crews and a C-130 crew that were preparing to fly home. While we coordinated radio communications and prepared to fly home, dawn was just beginning to show up in the skies over northern Laos. What makes this particular mission so unusual, in one sense, is that we almost never teamed up with other A-26 or FAC crews in Barrel Roll. Yet, there we were, teaming up with, and flying formation with, two other A-26 aircraft and a C-130 aircraft as dawn broke over the Plain of Jars. All of a sudden, all hell broke loose!!! I vividly remember reacting to a blinding flash of light and looking down from the right side of the cockpit. Tracers were flying all around us! The ground was black except for muzzle flashes and tracers from countless antiaircraft guns firing at us! When I looked down, I saw the entire ground area below us erupting in antiaircraft fire as we passed overhead. The air was full of tracers in all directions. I was in shock! I remember turning to Pappy and saying, "We can't fight this!" We had already dropped all of our ordnance. I also remember Pappy's lighted face and eyes showing a surprised "What the hell do you mean!" expression as we reacted to the unbelievably intense antiaircraft barrage. From previous Steel Tiger missions, I knew what eight to ten firing antiaircraft guns looked like, but this was something totally different. There must have been 100 or more antiaircraft guns firing at the same time. None of us had ever seen anything like it. Capt. Jay Norton and Capt. Roy Zarruchi were flying in one of the other A-26 aircraft that night. Hundreds, if not thousands, of tracers lit up the early morning sky. Looking back, one thing is clear. Something very big was happening from an enemy point of view in the Plain of Jars on July 1, 1968. I don't know what it was, but we felt very lucky to have survived the experience. It's a miracle none of our aircraft took a hit. Since we only had machine gun rounds left, we decided to return to base and live to fight another day. Our four aircraft joining up to fly formation must have been too much of a tempting target for the NVN gunners to resist, especially after Jay Norton and Roy Zarucchi rolled-in to check out what appeared to be a search light. We must have been silhouetted in the sky at the first light of dawn. As a result, we found ourselves positioned on the wrong end of an unbelievable cone of fire. That experience showed all of us that you can never let your guard down, even when you think the mission is over.

q. The Mission with USAFA Classmate "Mick" Roth

On the night of July 14, 1968, I had a memorable combat mission with Captain Mickey ("Mick") Roth, one of my classmates in the Class of 1963 at the Air Force Academy. Mick was a heavyweight at USAFA. He was our Cadet Wing Commander during our last year at the Academy. Lieutenant Colonel Francis McMullen was the navigator/co-pilot who normally flew with Mick but I filled in for Col. McMullen on that mission. Mick and Col. McMullen were the crew that gave me my formal combat ready check ride back on December 15, 1967 (my seventh mission). On the night of July 14, Mick and I were the only two crewmembers.

This was a memorable mission for three main reasons. First, Mick and I were on our own to fly and fight the mission that night. Second, it was a hot mission. Third, we felt the spirit of our common USAFA background at every stage of the flight.

The flight on July 14 was Mission No. 125 for me. It was probably Mission No. 150 or more for Mick. We were very experienced crewmembers at that point in time. We flew as if we had flown 1000 times together. Since we had flown so many combat missions in the A-26, our proficiency level could not have been higher. I believe it is fair to say that Mick and I were pleased to be on our own for the mission.

After we reached cruise altitude and checked in with Alley Cat, we were directed to link up with a C-123 Candlelight FAC crew in Steel Tiger. The C-123 crew had pinpointed the location of ten trucks on the Trail and was waiting for us to arrive on the scene. We went to work immediately. We destroyed six of the ten trucks and had six AAA guns shooting at us. The antiaircraft guns were very active and the tracers were coming very close to our aircraft. When our ordnance had been expended, we took up a westerly heading toward NKP. The C-123 crew was happy with the results.

The flight back to NKP was most enjoyable. There is nothing quite like the joy of doing your duty and being on the return trip to home base after kicking butt without any of the enemy bullets hitting you and your partner. That is the way Mick and I felt as we flew west toward the Mekong River and NKP. We definitely felt the spirit of our common USAFA background as we descended, lowered the gear, and gently touched down on the runway. I could not have asked for a more memorable mission with a USAFA classmate.

r. The "One Pass" Mission with Col. Brumm

This mission stands out in my memory because it was the only mission I can remember that we released all ordnance on just one pass. The date was July 23, 1968. This was Mission No. 132 for me. I had flown every night for the last five nights. We had gotten into a beehive of activity every night. Lieutenant Colonel Robert Brumm was the pilot in the left seat on the night of July 23. Colonel Brumm was our squadron commander between Col. Farmer and Col. Shippey. On the night of July 23, it was obvious that all hell was breaking loose, once again, as we approached the target area in Steel Tiger. We were about forty-five miles due east of NKP when it came our turn to put our ordnance on the truck traffic below. Numerous FAC and attack aircraft were operating in the target area with us. Tracers were flying everywhere. The radio chatter was non-stop. Bombs were detonating all along up and down the road structure. Col. Brumm made a command decision that we were going to put in all of our bombs on the first pass. Under the circumstances, that sounded like one hell of a good idea. "Roger," was my response. As he nosed over the aircraft, I reached over the throttles and announced, "Master Bomb Control Switch On," "Bomb Bay Doors coming open," and "I will walk the bombs off the wings." As we dived into the target area, I recall quickly and simultaneously pressing the switches downward for wing stations 1 and 8, then 2 and 7, then 3 and 6, and then 4 and 5. Tracers filled the air. The aircraft seemed to rapidly pause and jump as all of the ordnance departed the wing stations and bomb bay. As Col. Brumm quickly applied power, turned the aircraft away from the target area, and initiated a pullout from the dive, I flipped the switch to close the bomb bay doors. Then a most amazing thing happened. As Col. Brumm abruptly turned the aircraft to evade hostile fire, I happened to be directly facing the ground as our bombs struck the ground and detonated. It was an unbelievable sight. The bombs walked right down the road, crossed over a hilltop at a road intersection, and continued detonating among firing gun positions on both sides of the hilltop. The flashes from the detonating bombs lit up the entire target area. I was captivated by the sight. Talk about a once in a lifetime experience!

CHAPTER 10: THE JOY OF MEETING DIANNE IN HAWAII

I knew that after I had flown combat missions for more than six months I would be eligible to take military leave and meet Dianne in Hawaii. Needless to say, I hoped and prayed for that day to arrive. Anyone who has ever served in combat will tell you the same thing. The spouse you love and had to leave behind is the most important person in the world to you. Your spouse and family, and your religious convictions, are the foundation that sustains you. Dianne and I had only been married four years when I left home for the Vietnam War, and we were very much in love. Looking back, until about a month before my military leave was to begin, I was almost afraid to let myself believe that Dianne and I would really meet in Hawaii. At that point, I began to believe that I would survive at least long enough to meet Dianne in Hawaii. Finally, on July 28, 1968, Pappy and I flew our last mission before leave was to begin. I was ecstatic. The plan was for Pappy and me to go on leave and meet Dianne and Elaine (Pappy's wife) in Honolulu on August 3. Dianne and Elaine would take commercial airline flights from the States to Honolulu, and Pappy and I would take military hops to Honolulu to meet them. Pappy and I departed NKP for Bangkok aboard a C-130 on July 29. To our amazement, we made immediate military hop connections to Kadena, Okinawa, and then on to Hickham AFB, Hawaii. Because of gaining a day crossing the international dateline, Pappy and I actually arrived at Hickham AFB aboard a KC-135 at 4:30 a.m. on July 30. After spending that first night at the Hickham VOQ, Pappy and I relocated to Fort DeRussey in Honolulu (the Army Rest & Recuperation Center). We played golf and went to the beach every day waiting for Dianne and Elaine to arrive. We started feeling like human beings again, and we could hardly believe that Dianne and Elaine were on their way to meet us in Hawaii.

On the night of August 3, 1968, I met Dianne at the Honolulu International Airport, and it's a gross understatement to say that I was **excited**!!! Suddenly, as that **beautiful** creature stood right there in front of me once again, the last eight months of combat and loneliness evaporated into thin air. It was a magical moment. We were immediately into each other's arms and the hustle and bustle and strangeness of the airport simply melted away. We were in each other's arms once again and that was all that mattered. There are certain wonderful moments in life that your spirit and soul wish could last forever, and that was clearly one of those rare, wonderful moments. Dianne's philosophy in college was that you can only experience joy and happiness in proportion to the pain and suffering that you have experienced in life. For eight months, we experienced a lot of pain and suffering. On August 3, and for two weeks more, God allowed us to experience the true joy and happiness of being together again as man and wife in a paradise called Hawaii.

It was like the honeymoon we never really had the opportunity to take. After Pappy and I met Dianne and Elaine at the airport, we all drove out to Bellows Air Force Station in a rented car. We had reservations to spend the next six days in cottages directly on the beach. Other than being excited, I don't remember a thing about the trip from the airport to the Bellows beach cottages northeast of Honolulu. I do remember that the four us got together for a champagne toast after we arrived at the cottages. As I'm sure you can imagine, we soon retreated to our respective private cottages for the night. The next morning, Dianne was absolutely beautiful as she drew pictures and wrote messages in the sand outside our cottage. The ocean was a beautiful dark blue. The white foam on the top of the thunderous blue-green waves hitting the beach shimmered in the sun. The coarse brown sand in the waves, and just beyond the waves toward our cottage, made a perfect place to write and draw in the sand. I have a permanent memory in my mind of Dianne wearing a two-piece swimsuit (black and white checked with gold trim), looking forever young, beautiful, and tanned, writing and drawing in that sand. My recollection is that she wrote our names in big flowing letters in the sand—Roger, Dianne and Kimberly—and I believe she drew a big heart, like a Valentine's Day heart, beside our names. That was another very special moment in time.

We spent the next six days at the cottage at Bellows Air Force Station. It was a perfect setting to relax and unwind with the person you loved. We had never seen such a beautiful beach. The beach and ocean view were simply spectacular. Likewise, the tropical trees and the distant rippling mountain range were uncommonly beautiful. It seemed that the weather was always perfect, the sky was constantly blue with puffy white clouds, the ocean breeze was delightful, and the temperature was always in the 70s or 80s. The expression, "tropical paradise," took on a whole new meaning for us—we got to experience it for ourselves. During those six days, we visited Sea Life Park (a beautiful saltwater aquarium overlooking the vast Pacific Ocean) and the Polynesian Cultural Center (an interesting center showcasing heritage Polynesian dancing, food and village life). We also drove around Diamond Head and into Honolulu to see a new movie called, "The Graduate," starring Dustin Hoffman and Ann Bancroft.

On August 9, 1968, we checked out of Bellows AFS and drove into Honolulu, where we checked into the Outrigger Hotel. Both the hotel and Waikiki Beach were incredibly beautiful. I distinctly remember being with Dianne on the balcony outside our upper floor room. We were only twenty-six years old. We had just finished dressing for dinner. Dianne was tanned, happy, and beautiful beyond description. We took some photos. We soaked up the tropical beach scenery. We enjoyed a wonderful dinner and we settled in for one of the most incredible weeks of our lives—a full week at the Outrigger Hotel on Waikiki Beach. What more could any young couple in love hope for???!!!

During the next few days we lived life to the fullest. We visited beautiful Waikiki Beach at every opportunity. We soaked up the sun and absorbed the view. We ventured into the surf and even tried surfing (my surf board did not want to cooperate and I spent much more time falling off the board than standing on the board). We ate at many superb restaurants, including a sixteen story revolving restaurant.

We saw the Tommy Sands show, and "Mame," a musical starring Anne Southern. We took a Pearl Harbor tour. We even took a driving tour of the entire Island of Oahu with Chief Master Sergeant Marshall Wolcott (our volunteer tour guide) and Bobby and Elaine Sears. The driving tour included incredibly beautiful beaches, mountains, sugar cane and pineapple fields, and a visit to a sailplane launching and recovery airfield. But most of all, Dianne and I treasured each moment together. Alas, all good things must come to an end.

On August 16, we experienced the pain of saying goodbye. I was with Dianne when she boarded the 10:00 p.m. Pan American flight for home. I would have given anything to have been able to go home with her. We were most thankful for the time that we had just spent together. We were also very apprehensive about what the next three or four months might bring. Nevertheless, we knew our duty as we saw it. Dianne would fly back home, resume teaching and parenting responsibilities, and wait for me to return. I would fly back to NKP, resume combat flying operations, and wait for the day I could return to Dianne and Kimberly. However, as we found out, knowing our duty didn't make the pain any less agonizing.

CHAPTER 11: THE PSYCHOLOGY OF RETURNING TO THE WAR

This is a short chapter. I could have called it "The Pain of Returning to the Combat Zone." I'm sure Dianne felt exactly the same way. We both returned to our own form of combat zone. We didn't know if we would survive the next three months of the one-year assignment. If one of us didn't survive, that meant that "we" didn't survive. We both had tears forming in our eyes as the war once again pulled us from each other's arms…and as our respective aircraft departed in opposite directions in August of 1968. Pappy and I flew back to NKP via KC-135 and C-130 aircraft to Kadena AFB, Okinawa, and Bangkok and then on to NKP. On August 21, Pappy and I flew our next combat mission into Steel Tiger (Mission No. 137 for me)—the Monsoon (rainy) season was getting into high gear. We were forced to drop our ordnance under ground radar control. The next night, we found a hole in the clouds and dropped our ordnance on a pre-briefed target. We saw a lot of rain and lightning. The left engine quit on landing— otherwise a no-sweat mission. After landing, some of the guys in the squadron got pretty drunk and Major Mark Richards announced over the O' Club speaker system that the base was under attack (a joke) but everybody believed him and rushed out of the club, and the whole base ended up in a panic! Welcome back to NKP and the combat zone.

CHAPTER 12:
UNFORGETTABLE NIMRODS
AND A-26 COMBAT
MISSIONS (PART II)

a. The "Almost Bought the Farm" Mission with Major Peters

Have you ever found yourself in a situation that you thought you were going to die in the next instant? I have. The night was August 24, 1968, and it was Mission No. 140 for me. By that time, I was considered a seasoned veteran of flying combat missions in Steel Tiger and Barrel Roll. For that reason, I was teamed up with Major Elmer Peters, a new pilot in the squadron who had just completed his initial checkout rides in our operating area. My recollection is that this particular mission was the only time that Major Peters and I ever flew together. I recall that he was likeable, slender and somewhat intense. I imagine that he had about the same impression of me.

To get into the mission, I have strong memories of taking off and flying in terrible weather. It seemed that the Monsoon rainy season had really become entrenched and that we had our hands full just navigating and controlling the aircraft as we flew over the Steel Tiger road structure. We couldn't see anything but lightning, rain and dark clouds as we monitored the flight instruments and radios. I recall being concerned about managing our remaining fuel. We had flown in these conditions for what seemed like hours when Major Peters, all of a sudden and without any warning to me that I can remember, pushed the aircraft over into a steep dive. I remember scrambling to turn on the Master Bomb Control Switch and open the bomb bay doors. I recall seeing large white and red tracers coming up toward us from the ground at us as we dived down into a hole in the ominous, dark black clouds. The white and red tracers racing at us illuminated the hole and the surrounding grayish-black billowing clouds.

I couldn't see the ground. I recall rapidly calling out altitudes as we continued to press the attack…5000, 4500, 4000, 3500, 3000 feet…**HOLY $#?!** I then instantaneously shifted into full-blown emergency mode! I shouted, "pull up, pull up," but there was no obvious response. I don't believe there was time to slap Major Peters on his right shoulder—a signal to pull up. There seemed to be no response to my yells to pull up. For the first and only time in my experience as an A-26 navigator/co-pilot, I grabbed the flight control yoke in front of me and pulled back with everything that I had in me. I sensed that Major Peters joined me in pulling back on the control yoke. The aircraft shuddered and damn near came unglued. In that instant I recall seeing the altimeter unwinding through 2500 feet, the control column back in my lap, the aircraft shuddering to avoid a stall… and most of all…I recall my prayers as I looked into complete blackness and braced myself for what I thought was going to be the moment of instantaneous impact and death.

Somehow it didn't happen. Somehow we survived. I had flown into that same area many times before and I thought it was all over. I was waiting for the lights to go out. We seemed to be suspended in time. We pushed the throttles forward, and to my amazement, the aircraft continued flying and we started regaining airspeed and altitude. My navigation charts indicated that the terrain elevation at that location was 2200 feet. We must have bottomed out below 2200 feet. Maybe we bottomed out over a ravine. Maybe the charts were wrong. Maybe our altimeter setting was wrong. For whatever reason, Major Peters and I lucked out big time that night. We regained altitude and gave each other a knowing glance. We had cheated death. The unusually aggressive dive-bombing pass and lack of crew coordination before initiating the pass almost resulted in disaster. The horrible weather and low fuel reserves were major complicating factors. We gingerly dropped our remaining ordnance on the next pass and thankfully took up a westerly heading to return to NKP. Thank you, Jesus!!!

Elmer might have a different take on that mission. Certainly, the circumstances couldn't have been more challenging. He may have said something to me before initiating the dive that simply didn't register on me. The weather was terrible and we were bouncing all over the place. It was our first flight together, so we didn't have the opportunity to develop normal crew coordination. The dive had to be very steep to stay in the small hole that suddenly appeared in the billowing, black storm clouds. Since we were low on fuel, we needed to dump our ordnance load on a target at the first opportunity. I do know that Elmer became one of our best Nimrod pilots. We both learned some valuable lessons from our "almost bought the farm" mission over Laos on that unforgettable night back in August of 1968.

b. The B-57 "Hit in Mid-Air" Mission

We absolutely loved the B-57 Red Birds and Yellow Birds!!! I witnessed the professionalism and courage of the B-57 crews many times along the Ho Chi Minh Trail in 1967 and 1968. We liked them so much that we felt it was an honor when we were teamed up with them to strike targets along the Trail. The B-57 was a two-engine jet dive-bomber with a two-man crew—a pilot and a navigator. The B-57 and A-26 crews shared a common objective—attack and destroy enemy targets along the Ho Chi Minh Trail at night. In my experience, the A-26 and the B-57 combat aircraft and crews were our most effective nighttime attack aircraft and crews in the Steel Tiger area of operations.

On September 21, 1968, I flew a most unusual mission. That night I had the good fortune to fly with Captain Jack Bright, an Air Force Academy graduate and good friend whom I greatly admired. Jack Bright was the Cadet Squadron Commander of First Cadet Squadron during my sophomore (Third Class) year at the Academy. His nickname was "Lightnin," and his motto, according to the 1961 USAFA Yearbook, was "Sit down and think about it for awhile." According to the yearbook, Jack was from Cedar Rapids, Iowa. I really liked him. We all liked him. He was a class act.

My diary entry for September 21 indicates that Jack was in the left seat, Pappy was in the right seat, and I was in the jump seat behind Pappy. According to my diary, this was the first left-seat ride for Jack in the war. We checked in with Alley Cat and flew to our assigned target area. I distinctly remember flying into that particular target area. It was late nighttime and we were concentrating on the radio communications and the scene that unfolded below. Our Alley Cat instructions were to hold short of "Foxtrot," a particularly hot target location, while other strike aircraft hit the target. That was when it happened! It was nighttime and it was very dark. We took up the assigned altitude of about 7000 feet and flew in a clockwise direction around the assigned target area. We tuned into the same communications channel as a Blind Bat FAC aircraft and the B-57 strike aircraft.

I could not believe what I saw and heard as the B-57 crew went to work. As we observed the B-57 strike progression of events, and as we orbited the strike area and prepared to attack the target after the B-57 strike, I was hearing and seeing the B-57 crew strike the target. The B-57 crewmembers professionally communicated that they understood the strike directions, that they were in a dive-bombing pass on the target, and that they were pulling off after the pass. All of a sudden, the unexpected happened. I was looking directly at the ground fires in the target area. I saw the bright flashes of the bombs that were dropped from the B-57 as the bombs impacted the ground. I saw a beehive of antiaircraft tracers fly into the sky over the target area as the bombs detonated. I heard a member of the B-57 crew calmly report that they had delivered their ordnance and they were pulling off the target. At that moment, I actually saw a line of tracers impact the B-57 aircraft as it was pulling off the target. The line of tracers simply stopped in mid-air. A large flash of bright white light and sparks lit up the night sky over the target area. At the same moment, a calm voice came over the air from the B-57 crew. "We have taken a hit, we are shutting down one of our engines and we are taking up an easterly heading."

That is when I began to understand the professionalism of the B-57 Red Birds and Yellow Birds. After I saw the tracers hit the B-57 aircraft on the night of September 21, 1968, we continued to follow the radio communications of the B-57 crew. I had never seen such professionalism. Try to imagine the scene as the tracers actually hit the B-57 aircraft as it pulled off target. The sky suddenly lit up as the tracers connected with a point in the sky—the B-57 aircraft—and my stomach hit bottom. After that, we held our altitude, and monitored communications as the B-57 crew flew toward the east and out of the strike zone. We listened as the B-57 crew reported what happened after they were hit.

From the B-57 crew, very calmly, after they delivered their bombs, on target, in Steel Tiger, on September 21, 1968, "We have shut down one engine and we have a problem with the other engine"… "We may have to eject and we are heading east toward the Gulf of Tonkin." We listened for another fifteen minutes or so as the B-57 crew continued flying east. Each radio communication from the B-57 crew was more desperate than the last. It was obvious that they were nursing the one remaining but damaged engine as they struggled to stay airborne. We finally heard them calmly report that they were punching out over the Gulf of Tonkin. The bravery of that particular B-57 crew was beyond description. Their conduct and radio communications, after they were hit, exemplified the very best that we could ever ask from our fellow American fighting men. I was awed by their professionalism, courage, skill, and calmness in the face of a full-blown emergency!

Later, after we hit our assigned targets and landed back at NKP, we learned that the B-57 crew successfully ejected over the Gulf of Tonkin and both crewmembers were picked up by a U.S. destroyer. Yea!!!!!!!!!!! Jack also had a great mission. Despite the shock of seeing the B-57 crew take a hit, Jack calmly delivered our A-26 ordnance in the same target area. He was given credit for destroying one truck. I suspect he deserved a lot more credit than that. He dived into the same hornet's nest and made them pay! After that memorable mission, Jack and I flew many more A-26 missions as a crew in the fall of 1968. I thoroughly enjoyed flying with Jack; he quickly became one of our best.

c. The "Sparks on Your Feet" Mission with Jack Bright

On the night of October 7, 1968, Jack and I had another memorable mission. The first aircraft scheduled for pre-flight had all sorts of electrical and maintenance problems, but we made every effort to overcome those problems and fly our assigned mission. The last straw occurred after we completed the before take-off checklist. As we

81

pushed the throttles full forward and started the take-off roll, a huge ball of sparks struck our flight boots as we raced down the runway. Our immediate response, other than yelling at the top of our lungs, was to jerk the throttles all the way back and jump on the brakes. Fortunately, we were able to safely abort the flight and return to the flight line to pre-flight a second A-26 aircraft. In due time, at 3:30 a.m. local time, we accelerated down the runway and successfully pulled up the gear in that flightworthy A-26 aircraft. We flew some seventy miles southeast of NKP and struck our assigned target in the vicinity of Khe Sanh in South Vietnam. Our squadron had flown numerous missions in support of the U.S. Marines at Khe Sanh in 1968. After dropping our ordnance and completing our mission, we took up a westerly heading toward NKP. At that moment in time, the scene was unforgettable. As we approached the Mekong River and NKP, there was a full moon ahead of us and the sun was coming up behind us…an indescribably beautiful scene!

d. The "Game Over" Mission at NKP

For me personally, this was the most unforgettable mission of the war. On the night of October 25, 1968, I flew my 182nd and last mission of the Vietnam War. Not only was it my last mission, it was also the last mission for Lt. Colonel John Shippey (Squadron Commander), Major John Parrish (pilot), Captain Leroy Zarruchi (navigator/co-pilot) and Captain Richard Willems (navigator/co-pilot). In the true spirit of combat crewmembers, we flew a three-ship formation departing NKP, and after we hit our targets we joined up and flew a three-ship formation back to NKP. We landed in rapid succession. I clearly remember the scene as we taxied into our parking space at the end of the mission. As we approached our parking space, our taxi lights were on and the propellers were turning and catching the light as we turned into our parking space. As we shut down the churning engines we saw a wonderful sight. We pushed open the cockpit canopies on both sides of the aircraft and the entire Nimrod squadron greeted us. I remember looking out of the open canopy on my side of the aircraft, seeing a fire truck approach the aircraft, and seeing a lot of Nimrod pilots and navigators running toward our aircraft. I also remember shouting, "Game Over!!!" The Nimrods that greeted us in the middle of the night understood what I meant. We did not consider the war to be a game but all of us understood that we wanted to do our duty to help win the war, and God willing, survive the war and return to our loved ones. When we shouted "Game Over," we meant that we had flown our last combat mission and we were going home!

After we shut down our engines, the scene was pure bedlam. The fire truck hosed down everyone and everything in sight. The fire truck crew made certain that everyone completing his last mission received the full brunt of the water blasting out of the fire truck hoses. It was wonderful!!! I remember being thoroughly hosed down even before my feet touched ground while descending the aircraft ladder. Lights were flashing and everybody was yelling!!! I was soaked, and we were on our way to the O' Club for a celebration. I didn't fully comprehend it yet, but my combat tour was over. Somehow, by the grace of God, I had survived and I would soon be on my way back to Dianne and Kimberly—the family that I loved. We had a great celebration and party at the O' Club, but nothing could overshadow the true meaning of what had just happened. Much to my surprise and disbelief, God had allowed me to survive 182 A-26 combat missions in the Vietnam War. I don't have the words to describe what that felt like. I was ecstatic. I was numb. I was thankful. I was proud to be a Nimrod. But most of all, I knew that I had done my duty and that I would soon return to Dianne and Kimberly, and to the United States of America... to the family and the country that meant everything to me.

Nimrod Crew (1967-68): Major Bobby J. Sears (right) and Captain Roger D. Graham (left). Note that A-26 in photo has definitely seen a lot of combat time. Aircraft and crews out of NKP logged hundreds of missions in the 1966-69 time frame.

A-26A (B-26K) with full load of ordnance flying over SEA (1968). Note that only the code "TA" and the serial number (671) appears on the vertical tail section. No U.S. insignia was depicted on these U.S. Nimrod aircraft because the aircraft and crews were part of the "Secret War in Laos."

Another view of same A-26A Counter Invader in vicinity of NKP (1968).

Still another view of the A-26A with full ordnance load and Mekong River in background.

Crews of the 609th Special Operations Squadron in front of an A-26A in 1968 at Nakhon Phanom Royal Thai Air Force Base, Thailand. Note truck "kills" depicted under the cockpit. Lt. Colonel John J. Shippey, Squadron Commander, stands at far right beside nose wheel. On Wing, Left to Right: Capt. Jay Norton, Capt. Thomas Owens, Major Robert Bennett, Major Robert Squires, Capt. Thomas Bronson, Major Mark Richards, Capt. Frank Nelson, Major Bryant Murray, Major Walter Langford, Capt. Michael Roth, Capt. Seijun Tengan. Standing at Ground Level, Left to Right: Major Douglas Carmichael, Major Bobby Sears, Major Loren Gierhart, Lt. Col. Francis McMullen, Major Bernard Disteldorf, Capt. Richard Willems, Major Robert Zimmerman, Major Kenneth LaFave (on ascent ladder just below canopy), Capt. Michael Henry, Major Bennie Heathman, Major Douglas Hawkins, Capt. Bruce Wolfe, Lt. Col. John Shippey.

Another photo of the A-26A crews in 1968 time frame. <u>Front row, left to right</u>: Major Delbert Litton, Major Walter Langford, Major Robert Bennett, Major Loren Gierhart, Capt. Thomas Bronson, Capt. William Cohen, Major Kenneth LaFave, Major Robert Squires, Capt. Roger Graham, Capt. Lawrence Elliott. <u>Back row, standing, left to right</u>: Major Bobby Sears, Capt. Don Maxwell, Major Edward Robinson, Major Douglas Carmichael, Capt. Ernest Weidenhoff, Major Mark Richards, Capt. Leroy Zarucchi, Lt. Col. Francis McMullen, Lt. Col. Robert Brumm, Lt. Col. Atlee Ellis, Capt. Michael Roth, Capt. Jay Norton, Major Daniel Grob, Capt. Chuck Kenyon.

Another photo of crews of the 609th Special Operations Squadron in front of an A-26A (1968). <u>On Wing, Left to Right</u>: Capt. Chuck Kenyon, Major Dan Grob, Major Walt Langford, Major Del Litton, Capt. Roy Zarucchi, Capt. Don Maxwell, Major Bob Bennett, Capt. Tom Bronson, Capt. Lawrence Elliott, Capt. Mick Roth, Capt. Roger Graham, Capt. Jay Norton. <u>Standing at Ground Level, Left to Right</u>: Capt. Ernest Weidenhoff, Major Mark Richards, Major Ed Robinson, Lt. Col. Francis McMullen, Lt. Col. Bob Brumm, Major Ken LaFave, Major Loren Gierhart, Capt. Bill Cohen, Major Doug Carmichael, Lt. Col. Atlee Ellis, Major "Pappy" Sears, Major Bob Squires.

CHAPTER 13: THE JOY OF RETURNING TO THE FAMILY

Needless to say, it was pure joy for me to rejoin my family after the long flight home. For everyone who has had the experience, the flight across the Pacific Ocean is a very long flight. It seemed that the aircraft and its engines would drone on forever, but after what truly seemed like forever, my flight finally arrived in California in late November, 1968. My recollection is that I stayed overnight in California before proceeding on to Princeton, West Virginia, where Dianne and Kimberly were staying with Billie, Dianne's mother. My joy at arriving in California was dampened by what I saw and heard. To me, the television news programs seemed anti-war and anti-American. Many of the civilians I encountered seemed unfriendly and anti-American. I shrugged it off because I did not want to dwell on anything negative—after all, I had just finished my combat tour and I was on my way home to rejoin the family I loved!

My actual arrival back in Virginia and West Virginia was most unusual. Just prior to Thanksgiving Day in 1968, I was scheduled to fly commercial flights to Roanoke, Virginia, and then on to the Mercer County Airport near Princeton, West Virginia. I had called Dianne and asked her to meet my flight at the Mercer County Airport. Much to our surprise, a major, early winter snowstorm arrived in the Roanoke and Princeton area just before my flight arrived at Roanoke. The snowstorm prevented my flight from departing Roanoke for the Mercer County Airport. In the meantime, Dianne was attempting to drive in a dangerous nighttime snowstorm to meet me at the Mercer County Airport. The airline I was flying with made arrangements for me to be transported to Princeton by van and when I arrived at the house at Princeton, nobody was home. After several hours of frustration, we all reunited at the house in Princeton, and it was a great joy for all to finally be together again after a long year of pain and separation.

I would like to say that everything was perfect in the days that followed, but everything was not perfect. Dianne was perfect—she was as beautiful and wonderful as ever. Kimberly was perfect—she was now three years old and she was even more beautiful and wonderful than I had remembered. Dianne's mother, Billie, was perfect—she was a beautiful and wonderful Christian woman who I dearly loved and admired. I soon realized that what was not perfect was me. I smoked too much, drank alcohol too much, and used profanity far too much. The funny thing is…I thought I was normal…until I suddenly left my Nimrod buddies and rejoined normal society. I didn't realize it then, but I do now; it would take a lifetime to try to return to "normal." Despite those challenges, it was still a real joy to return to Dianne, Kimberly and family life!!!

Dianne, Kimberly and I didn't have long to rebuild our family relationship. Immediately after Thanksgiving Day, 1968, we departed in our car for Riverside, California. I knew that I was going to be reassigned to a B-52 unit following the Vietnam War A-26 assignment, and I requested any B-52 squadron on the East Coast. The Air Force response was to assign me to a B-52 squadron at March Air Force Base, California. If you have been a career military family, you appreciate the humor. You get the opposite of what you ask for. In any event, the assignment to March AFB turned out to be a good one. We rented a nice two-bedroom home in Riverside, just across the street from Marie and John Perrone, a young couple with a strong Italian heritage. We very much enjoyed Riverside and the B-52 assignment, and our friendship with the Perrone family, but we knew that we would soon be leaving for Morgantown, West Virginia, where I had been accepted in our home state for law school at West Virginia University (WVU). I passed the Law School Admission Test in Bangkok in the midst of flying A-26 combat missions out of Nakhon Phanom RTAFB, Thailand. Most important, we learned that our second daughter, Kristine Marie (Kristi) had been conceived in the spring of 1969.

I resigned from the Air Force in late summer 1969 and we

completed the automobile trip from Riverside to Morgantown in August of 1969. We were fortunate to find a nice three-bedroom house to rent in Morgantown as I registered for law school at WVU in the fall of 1969. I was not prepared for the tumultuous anti-war demonstrations that we witnessed on the WVU campus in 1969. You need to understand that I still felt like a member of the U.S. military forces. To my dismay, TV and radio broadcasts were full of anti-war media coverage. I thought that the media had completely missed the real story. To me, the media only covered, and only dwelt upon, anything and everything that diminished or attacked the efforts of the U.S. Government in the Vietnam War, or the extraordinary efforts of our military forces in the war. In my first semester of law school, I was totally amazed that my Criminal Law professor announced that an anti-war demonstration was about to take place right outside the law school and that everyone was excused to leave class and join the anti-war demonstration. I clearly recall getting up from my desk and approaching the Criminal Law professor. As some 95% of my 130 law school classmates walked outside to join in the smoke and chaos of the anti-war protesters, I told my Criminal Law professor that I had just returned from a combat tour in the Vietnam War; that I did not agree with the anti-war protesters; that I had paid my tuition and fees; and that I expected to attend a Criminal Law class that day. Would you like to know what happened? We only had about seven or eight students in attendance, but we did have class that day.

That was just one example of what was taking place across the country. Our nation was in complete turmoil. If significant numbers of students at a university in a small, conservative state like West Virginia could demonstrate against the war, imagine what the rest of the country looked like. It was a scene of pure rebellion and chaos. Brave men and women were not nearly as vocal as the anti-war protesters. It was difficult to distinguish genuine conscientious objectors from draft dodgers. In any event, large numbers of draft dodgers were in full flight to Canada or beyond. Much of the media in the United States, unwittingly or not, became a tool of the North Vietnamese communists who were planning and executing widespread military aggression in South Vietnam (e.g. the Tet Offensive in January 1968). The media coverage dwelt at great length on the My Lai atrocity committed by a few Army troops, and gave almost no coverage to more widespread atrocities committed by North Vietnamese troops and Viet Cong guerrillas. It seemed that movie actress Jane Fonda got more positive American media coverage while sitting in a North Vietnamese antiaircraft gun in Hanoi than several hundred American combat aviators who were being tortured and mistreated as POWs in the nearby "Hanoi Hilton." It was probably the first time in American history that the American media failed to fully support the U.S. Government and U.S. military forces in time of war. The communists were very astute in using the American media to their advantage.

While in law school at West Virginia University in the fall of 1969, I remember a radio call-in program from Pittsburgh in which a young woman was railing against the war, the U.S. Government and the U.S. military, and inviting callers to join in the verbal attack. From Morgantown, I dialed the station number and was immediately on-air. I explained to her that I had just served with the Nimrods in the war and that I thought that she and her station had it all wrong. I was on the phone but I could hear my voice on the radio. I explained my position. On-air, she went dead silent. To me, that was a defining moment. Personally, I was dismayed at the chaos in America when I returned home from the war. I was of the opinion that if Americans had known what was really going on in Southeast Asia, they would have opposed the communists in North and South Vietnam, and they would literally have moved heaven and earth to support our U.S. military forces and allies in South Vietnam. Unfortunately, that did not happen.

CHAPTER 14: LASTING IMPRESSIONS

Like every American who served in our military forces during the Vietnam War, I have many lasting impressions. Even more than we realized at the time, the combat experience was so intense that it followed us the rest of our lives. That war experience was a real test of us as individuals, and us as a nation. Personally, I believe that our U.S. military men and women fared far better as individuals than we did as a nation.

As I write the closing chapters of this book, I salute the Nimrods. What an incredible brotherhood of U.S. Air Force combat aviators and patriots! I also salute all Air Force, Marine Corps, Navy and Army veterans who served in the Vietnam War. It was not a happy time. It was a time of "Duty, Honor, Country." We served our country, we performed our duty, and we pray that we served with honor. But before continuing with my last impressions, I would like to discuss the psychology of flying combat missions in the Vietnam War.

Part I: The Psychology of Flying Combat Missions in the Vietnam War

As I reflect back on the Vietnam War combat flying experience, probably the central recollection has to do with the psychological reaction of American military combat crewmembers, including myself, as we fought our way through the psychological phases of combat aviation. I believe that other crewmembers in my squadron would generally agree that we experienced four distinct psychological phases in combat flying.

The phases are distinct in my mind, and I will attempt to describe each of the four phases.

First Phase: The first phase involved the initial combat checkout rides, and roughly the first 25 combat missions with the pilot and navigator/co-pilot assigned to any given crew. The initial combat checkout rides were intended to familiarize all crewmembers with the area of operations (primarily Steel Tiger and Barrel Roll), and to expose crewmembers to the extreme demands of actual combat (they are trying to kill you, you are trying to kill them first). My recollection is that our training prepared us to be top-notch A-26 attack dive-bomber crewmembers, but our training did not really prepare us to face the psychological demands of the Vietnam War. As we mechanically flew the first six or seven familiarization missions with seasoned crewmembers, we were ready to fly the aircraft and attack the targets; however, we were not really ready for the psychological reality that we might not survive the war. That reality hit me big-time! I am a fairly logical thinker. After my initial combat checkout rides, I thought that the odds were definitely against surviving a full year of flying A-26 combat missions. During the early combat missions, I had the feeling that all of the tracers from the antiaircraft artillery (AAA) guns were coming directly at me. Despite the initial realization that the odds did not look good for surviving a full year of A-26 combat flying, I consciously decided that I was in it for the long run, and that with all of my Air Force Academy training, flight training, and personal commitment, there was really no honorable alternative but to stay the course and do everything within my power to help fight and win the war.

Second Phase: The second phase involved becoming proficient combat crewmembers, and becoming even more determined to do our part to help win the war. About the 30th combat mission, I was thankful that I was still alive, and I was happy that Pappy and I were becoming highly proficient combat crewmembers. Major Sears and I became a more effective combat crew with each and every successive combat mission. I believe that Pappy and I discovered the optimum approach for combat flying. We were aggressive but we did not take unnecessary chances. Our combat flying experience showed us that it did not pay to be stupidly aggressive, or to be frozen with fear. Pappy and I did our homework. We knew the enemy area of operations and we knew enemy tactics. We mastered the checklists and procedures associated with successfully flying the A-26, and crew coordination became second nature. Finally, we mastered the art of coordinated combat operations with other FAC and attack aircraft. In short, between the 30th and 75th missions, we became a highly effective combat crew. In this phase, we were the enemy's worst nightmare. We were highly proficient, and we were intent on inflicting maximum casualties and damage on the enemy. More than anything else, we wanted to win the war.

Third Phase: Frankly, at the beginning of the third phase, I was somewhat surprised that I was still alive. The third phase started at about the time of the 75th combat mission. At that point in time, I was convinced that we had arrived at becoming one of the most proficient and effective U. S. combat crews in the entire Vietnam War. Although the prospect of every combat mission instilled more dread, we knew that with every mission we were becoming that much more of an efficient killing-machine. My reaction at that point in time was something that I had never anticipated. I actually began to feel sorry for the enemy soldiers we were killing. Although I personally did not agree with communist fighters taking over Southeast Asia, I felt absolutely no joy in knowing that I was part of a fighting force that was effectively destroying countless enemy lives. We took off, we flew, and we attacked whatever targets presented themselves. We were confident, and we attacked and destroyed countless truck convoys, gun positions, enemy troop positions and enemy storage positions. With increased proficiency and confidence, I was able to distinguish between life-threatening situations and routine air strikes. For example, during night strike missions I began to distinguish between tracers that were really close to striking our aircraft, and tracers that were far enough from our aircraft to pose no real threat. The red and white tracers that came really close became very large and bright as they flashed by the cockpit. The tracers that were not as close were relatively shorter and not as bright. Other than the tracers, we had to constantly remain vigilant to avoid mid-air collisions with friendly aircraft, and to avoid impacting the ground during dive-bombing passes.

Fourth Phase: The fourth phase involved a renewed hope for survival. As I flew the 100th mission and beyond, I skeptically began to believe that I might have a chance to survive the war! We continued preparing for and completing mission after mission, and the number of completed combat missions into Laos and Vietnam kept getting higher and higher. At that point, as my one-year tour neared ending in October of 1968, I dared think that I might survive and rejoin Dianne and Kimberly in the good old U.S.A. It finally happened! When I completed my 182nd combat mission on October 25, 1968, my tour of duty was over! I will never forget the exhilarating feeling of relief as the aircraft taxied into the parking area after that mission and we cut the engines. The best part was the realization that soon I was going to experience the unbelievable, the incredible, and the indescribable joy of once again being with Dianne and Kimberly, my family, back in the United States of America!!!

Part II: Lingering Last Impressions

There are many lingering last impressions of the Vietnam War experience. The experience meant many different things to different people. At the time of my A-26 assignment in the Vietnam War in 1967-68, my understanding of the war was that the communist North Vietnamese government, supported by the Soviet Union and China, was intent on securing a military victory against the South Vietnamese government and thereby unite all of Vietnam under the North Vietnam communist government. The Cold War foreign policy of the United States at the time was to oppose communist expansionism around the globe, by military force if necessary, and to support democratic governments threatened by the communists. Our policy-makers, beginning with Presidents Truman and Eisenhower, sought to contain communism, and feared that the communists might take over one country after another (the "domino theory") unless the United States stepped in to help threatened friendly countries oppose communism.

Our military involvement in Vietnam began under President John Kennedy's administration in the early 1960s. President Kennedy gave the graduation address when my class graduated from the Air Force Academy in June 1963. I remember the excitement when his limousine entered Falcon Stadium, and I remember his incredible charisma as he stood waving in the limousine and the sunlight reflected off his face and reddish-looking hair. He was an incredibly dynamic speaker. I remember him challenging America's astronauts to reach the moon by the end of the decade, and I remember him challenging my class to protect the military interests of the United States around the globe. I also remember him addressing the nuclear and conventional military risks posed by the Soviet Union, and the challenges of communism and associated unconventional military operations in third world countries. He probably made some reference to the situation in Vietnam, but if he did, I must admit that I don't have any strong recollection of what he said. At the time, the conflict in Vietnam seemed distant and relatively insignificant. The members of my graduating class had no idea that most of us would soon become personally embroiled in an escalating war in Southeast Asia.

Not long after I began flying A-26 combat missions out of NKP in 1967, I began doubting if our U.S. civilian and military leaders were pursuing an effective military strategy to win the war. I could see that we were losing a lot of U.S. aircraft on tactical combat missions with limited military objectives. I knew that U.S. and South Vietnamese ground forces were taking a lot of casualties in combat operations in South Vietnam. It was obvious that U.S. and South Vietnamese ground forces were not involved in any offensive operations in North Vietnam or Laos, but at the same time, it was obvious that NVN and Viet Cong forces were constantly engaged in offensive operations in South Vietnam, Laos and Cambodia. I wondered why U.S. and South Vietnamese troops were not involved in any offensive actions in North Vietnam. I also wondered why U.S., South Vietnamese and friendly Laotian troops were not deployed to block the Ho Chi Minh Trail. A logical place for U.S. and allied ground troops to have blocked truck traffic on the Trail would have been in the area south of the Mu Gia Pass and west of Khe Sanh. U.S. air power from Thailand would have been very effective in close air support of U.S. and allied troops. Such a military strategy would have ended the flow of supplies to NVN and Viet Cong forces in the south, and would likely have resulted in a military victory for the U.S. and its allies. It would also have run the risk of direct military intervention by China or the Soviet Union.

I thought at the time that our national leaders must be pursuing a limited war strategy because of concern that the Soviet Union, or China, or both, might intervene directly in combat operations in the war if our military forces should suddenly be employed to cut the Trail, or mount a ground and naval offensive (in addition to the ongoing air offensive) in North Vietnam.

I didn't need to guess about U.S. military strategy for long. Early in 1968, I recall being one of many combat crewmembers attending a briefing at NKP given by a U.S. Air Force four-star general. The thing I remember most about his briefing is that he matter-of-factly stated that the U.S. was pursuing a strategy of attrition in the Vietnam War. That statement, coming from one of our senior military commanders, hit me like a ton of bricks. The room became very quiet when he made that comment. As combat crewmembers, we were stunned. At the time, the rapid U.S. military buildup in South Vietnam had reached approximately 500,000 troops, with approximately another 45,000 airmen in Thailand. It was sobering to realize that our military strategy was simply to maintain the status quo and kill enough enemy soldiers so that they would either give up or have insufficient numbers to continue meaningful military operations. For me personally, and for all of the combat crewmembers in the room, that meant that we could expect to continue flying dangerous combat missions, entailing great risks, with limited objectives. As American fighting men, that concept went against our grain. What we really wanted was to be a part of a military strategy that combined U.S. ground, air and naval strengths in a way that defeated the enemy in the shortest period of time. Unfortunately, such a military strategy never materialized.

To our amazement, what happened was that our national leaders made a decision to halt all bombing of North Vietnam between November 1, 1968 and April 6, 1972 (except for reconnaissance flights and "protective reaction" strikes). The North Vietnamese used the bombing pause to strengthen their positions on all fronts.

After my A-26 combat tour was over in November of 1968, I returned home to a country in near rebellion. Negative media coverage of the stalled war, and the great public outcry (particularly on college campuses across the country) against the war, convinced President Johnson not to run for re-election in the Presidential campaign of 1968.

President Nixon was elected largely on his campaign promise to end the war. In an effort to force North Vietnam to the negotiating table, President Nixon authorized resumed bombing of North Vietnam from May 10 to October 23, 1972 (Operation Linebacker I). When truce negotiations stalled, President Nixon authorized massive B-52 air strikes on Hanoi and Haiphong from December 18-29, 1972 (Operation Linebacker II). In my opinion, Linebacker II constituted the first and only major shift in U.S. military strategy in the war. Although B-52 losses were heavy in Linebacker II, the operation devastated Hanoi and Haiphong and quickly brought North Vietnam back to the negotiating table. If such massive air strikes on Hanoi and Haiphong had been authorized by President Johnson or President Nixon earlier in the war, the result could have been a military victory for the U.S. and its allies. In any event, Linebacker II led to a cease-fire agreement being signed in Paris on January 27, 1973. The cease-fire was signed by representatives of the United States, South Vietnam, North Vietnam and the Viet Cong. On February 12, 1973, 591 American POWs were released from North Vietnam prisons. Among them was John Borling, my good friend and Air Force Academy classmate, who had been shot down more than six years earlier during an F-4 mission over North Vietnam. The Laotians signed a cease-fire agreement on February 21, 1973. (Correll, John T., "The Vietnam War Almanac," **Air Force Magazine**, September 2004.)

As a result of the cease-fire, U.S. military forces were withdrawn from South Vietnam in 1973. By June 1973, only forty-nine U.S. military members (from all Services) remained in South Vietnam. However, more than 42,000 U.S. service members remained in Thailand. The North Vietnamese leadership played a waiting game, and in April of 1975 unleashed thirty divisions of NVN troops in a massive military invasion of South Vietnam. Although North Vietnamese leaders blatantly violated the "Agreement on Ending the War and Restoring Peace in Vietnam," Congress refused to authorize U.S. military re-engagement in South Vietnam and Saigon fell to North Vietnamese forces on April 30, 1975. Laos and Cambodia also quickly fell under communist control. Since more than 40,000 U.S. military personnel remained in Thailand, the communist leaders stopped short of any attempt to invade and conquer Thailand.

For most Americans, crucial American leadership decisions didn't come to light until years after the war ended. In his book, *Patriots*,[3] published in 2003, Christian Appy includes a telling interview of Charles Cooper, a U.S. Marine major (in 1965) who attended a Joint Chiefs of Staff briefing to President Johnson in the White House in November of 1965. During that briefing, General Wheeler, the Chairman of the Joint Chiefs of Staff, proposed mining Haiphong harbor, blockading the rest of the North Vietnam coastline, and simultaneously beginning a B-52 bombing offensive on Hanoi. The basic idea was to use U.S. principal naval and air strengths to quickly force North Vietnam to sue for peace (and thereby avoid the risk of becoming involved in a protracted Asian ground war). When the Chiefs from the Services all agreed with the proposed military strategy, Johnson exploded and started shouting obscenities. Cooper recalled that Johnson used the following language in the tirade. "You goddamn fucking assholes. You're trying to get me to start World War III with your idiotic bullshit—your 'military wisdom.'" Cooper related that Johnson erupted again later in the meeting. "The risk is just too high. How can you fucking assholes ignore what China might do? You have just contaminated my office, you filthy shitheads. Get the hell out of here right now." (For the full text of Charles Cooper's interview, see *Patriots*, pages 121-23.)

Christian Appy's *Patriots* also includes the key interview of Walt Rostow, President Johnson's national security adviser from 1966 to 1968. Rostow was considered one of the leading "hawks" in the Kennedy and Johnson administrations. As a young officer in World War II, he helped select bombing targets and gained high confidence in the effectiveness of airpower. The Rostow interview is most interesting because it reveals that on April 27, 1967, Rostow made fundamentally different military strategy recommendations to the President, the Joint Chiefs of Staff, and Secretaries Rusk and McNamara. Rostow recommended that U.S. ground forces enter Laos at the eighteenth parallel to cut the Ho Chi Minh Trail, thereby blocking crucial supplies from reaching communist forces south of that line in Laos, Cambodia and South Vietnam. Instead of being bogged down in a war of

---

[3] Appy, Christian G., *Patriots: The Vietnam War Remembered From All Sides*, Viking, 2003.

attrition, he anticipated that cutting the Trail would have forced North Vietnam to mass their ground forces against our forces on the Trail, where he believed we could have won a strategic victory by supporting our ground troops with concentrated heavy artillery and massive aerial bombing. In addition, Rostow wanted to use U.S. amphibious forces to take the North Vietnamese coastal city of Vinh hostage until Ho Chi Minh agreed to withdraw communist forces from South Vietnam and Cambodia. President Johnson rejected Rostow's recommendations, fearing that sending U.S. troops into North Vietnam or Laos would draw China directly into the war. Johnson and Secretary Rusk were greatly influenced by the entrance of China into the Korean War, and didn't want to risk the same thing happening in the Vietnam War. Rostow argued that the Vietnam War was different from Korea because his recommendations would not take U.S. forces closer than two or three hundred miles from the Chinese border, and he believed that North Vietnam didn't want China or the Soviet Union to become overtly involved in the war. Rostow thought it was rational to believe the North Vietnamese could not beat us if we cut the Ho Chi Minh Trail. Rostow disagreed with Johnson but respected the tough decisions Johnson had to make. China and the Soviet Union were both nuclear powers. According to Rostow, Johnson said over and over again that the alternative to what he was doing was a larger war and quite possibly a nuclear war. Johnson did not want to take that risk for America and for the human race. (For the full text of Walt Rostow's interview, see *Patriots*, pages 124-27.)

With the revelations contained in Cooper and Rostow's interviews, it's clear why U.S. military forces were restrained from invading North Vietnam or cutting the Ho Chi Minh Trail in Laos. Johnson and Rusk did not want to risk direct Chinese troop intervention of the sort that happened in Korea, and they did not want to risk the possibility of nuclear war with either the Soviet Union or China. As a result, the war of attrition stretched all the way into the Nixon era. By that time, the American public was polarized and appalled by the war and Nixon felt immense political pressure to extricate the U.S. from the war. Nixon was shrewd to visit China as a prelude to aggressively pursuing peace talks in Paris. When the peace talks stalled, Nixon was bold enough to authorize Linebacker II, the massive B-52 bombing of Hanoi and

Haiphong in December of 1972 that is credited with convincing the North Vietnamese and Viet Cong to resume negotiations and sign the cease-fire agreement in Paris on January 27, 1973.

North Vietnam suffered huge losses (some three million North Vietnamese killed in the war), and an estimated one million South Vietnamese were killed in the war. According to U.S. military records, a total of 47,378 American battle deaths occurred in the Vietnam War. Those statistics clearly show that the strategy of attrition resulted in enormous casualties for all participants in the war. Long after U.S. involvement in the war ended, some North Vietnamese veterans commented that the U.S. almost had the war won when we signed the cease-fire agreement and withdrew our forces. Despite heavy losses, the North Vietnamese people were united and patient...not true for the American side. (See generally, Correll, John T., "The Vietnam War Almanac," **Air Force Magazine**, September 2004.)

The end result was that North Vietnamese military forces invaded and conquered South Vietnam on April 30, 1975. U.S. forces did not suffer a military defeat at the hands of the North Vietnamese and Viet Cong communists. That could not have happened. However, U.S. forces were withdrawn from South Vietnam by June of 1973. While it's true that U.S. forces did not suffer defeat at the hands of the communists, it's also true that U.S. forces did not defeat North Vietnamese forces during the course of the Vietnam War. Clearly, U.S. forces could have defeated North Vietnamese forces in short order if they had been allowed to do so by U.S. national leaders. That didn't happen because U.S. leaders were unwilling to risk a larger war possibly involving large-scale Chinese troop intervention, and possibly involving nuclear war with China or the Soviet Union. After Saigon fell, Laos and Cambodia also fell under communist control.

You have to wonder if any nation really "won" the Vietnam War. Ho Chi Minh died in 1969, so he did not get to see the end of the war. General Giap, probably the most effective North Vietnamese military leader in what he called the "American War," described the American War as the most atrocious conflict in human history. If so, Ho Chi Minh and General Giap deserve their share of responsibility for that atrocious conflict. They refused to be content with an independent communist state in North Vietnam and they insisted on invading and taking over

South Vietnam and Laos regardless of the cost in human lives. General Westmoreland's search and destroy tactics were ineffective. He wanted to use U.S. troops to cut the Ho Chi Minh Trail west of Khe Sanh, but President Johnson did not want to take that risk. The leaders in South Vietnam and Laos were never effective in uniting their people and military forces to oppose communism in a meaningful way. The Vietnam War essentially destroyed President Johnson—he wanted to concentrate on his Great Society agenda, but the Vietnam War almost completely dominated his entire tenure as President. President Nixon didn't fare much better. He came under intense political pressure to end American involvement in the Vietnam War, and soon thereafter was destroyed by the Watergate scandal. The cost in terms of lives lost and lives ruined defies human understanding. For every individual that lost his or her life in the war, a family continued to suffer the loss of the loved one long after the war officially ended. Wounded veterans kept their physical and psychological scars with them for the rest of their lives. Even the physical destruction of land, buildings and other property involved long-term consequences.

If you want to be an American optimist, you can take some solace in the fact that America took a stand against communist aggression and expansionism. The domino effect stopped with South Vietnam, Laos and Cambodia. Thailand, Malaysia, Indonesia and Singapore remain non-communist and independent to this day. Since I was based at Nakhon Phanom RTAFB, Thailand, and since I greatly admired the spirit of independence and freedom of the Thai people, I take great joy that my role in the Nimrods helped Thailand remain an important ally free of communist domination. I do deeply regret that the Hmong people, the great mountain freedom fighters of northern Laos, were essentially wiped out by the North Vietnam and Pathet Lao communists after the fall of South Vietnam. Fortunately, many Hmong men, women and children escaped to Thailand or the United States. (For an excellent article on the Hmong and Barrel Roll operations, see Boyne, Walter J., "The Plain of Jars," **Air Force Magazine**, June 1999.)

As I reflect back on the Vietnam War, I am thankful to have been a survivor of that atrocious conflict. My father, Frank Graham, did not survive the atrocious conflict called World War II. I was only two years old when he was killed in action in the Battle of the Bulge in Belgium.

The date was January 5, 1945, and he was killed approximately 2 miles east of Bastogne. Although he was thirty-two years old at the time, and had three small children, he was drafted into the U.S. Army. The impact of his death on my mother, Dorothy, must have been devastating. Not only did she lose her husband, she was left to raise three small children (Shirley, Daniel and me) by herself. I am thankful that I survived the Vietnam War and that Dianne did not have to suffer that same experience. Our daughter, Kimberly, was three years old when I returned home from the Vietnam War. As the years passed, Dianne and I were blessed with two more wonderful children, Kristi and Ryan, and with three wonderful grandchildren, Colette, Averi and Chase (Kristi's children with husband Bill Visage). We know that we have much to be thankful for, and we realize that many families were not so fortunate.

Looking back, my impression is that there were two key pivotal points in time with regard to American involvement in the Vietnam War. The first key point had to do with President Johnson's decision to greatly increase American military troop strength in Vietnam between 1965 and 1968. At the end of 1964, we had 23,310 U.S. service members in South Vietnam, and another 6500 in Thailand. At the end of 1968, we had 536,134 U.S. service members in South Vietnam, and another 47,631 in Thailand. (See "The Vietnam War Almanac," cited above.) Some historians believe that troop buildup decision by Johnson was one of the biggest mistakes ever made by an American president. Ironically, President Johnson was not a "hawk" with regard to the war. He would have preferred to pursue his Great Society agenda in the United States. The wisdom of his troop buildup decision, coupled with his war of attrition strategy, would make a good debate.

In my judgment, the second key pivotal decision point had to do with Walt Rostow's recommendation on April 27, 1967, for the president to authorize U.S. troops to cut the Ho Chi Minh Trail. That was the right point in time to seriously consider such a recommendation. It did not entail direct confrontation with China or the Soviet Union (in contrast to the earlier recommendation by General Wheeler and the Joint Chiefs of Staff to mine Haiphong harbor, blockade the North Vietnam coast, and use B-52s to bomb Hanoi). The buildup of U.S. troop strength in South Vietnam, and Air Force strength in Thailand, placed U.S. forces in a position to cut the Trail and provide massive strike aircraft close air support to U.S. ground forces. If the president had authorized U.S. troops to cut the Trail, and assuming China and the Soviet Union did not escalate their involvement, I believe that U.S. forces would have successfully cut the Trail and won the war. On the other hand, if the President had authorized U.S. troops to cut the Trail, and several hundred thousand Chinese troops had entered the conflict, the President probably would have had no choice but to resort to the use of nuclear weapons or immediately withdraw U.S. troops. Again, the wisdom of this second key decision by President Johnson would make a good debate.

The lessons learned from the Vietnam War should be and are the subject of separate studies. However, the following lessons learned stand out like a beacon. Our national civilian and military leaders need to carefully pick and choose which conflicts warrant U.S. military involvement. Our national civilian and military leaders need to understand our actual and potential adversaries and only fully commit U.S. military forces when a clear, executable military strategy has been formulated and approved that logically and realistically leads to victory. If that cannot be done, barring a direct threat to the U.S., the U.S. should stay out of the conflict. Congress must step up to its responsibilities under the U.S. Constitution. We must not underestimate the willpower and capabilities of our potential or actual enemies. We need to maintain strong alliances with other friendly countries. Our national leaders and our allies must continue to strongly oppose terrorism, in all of its forms, and the spread of nuclear weapons. If U.S. military forces are committed to a conflict, the U.S. Government and the American public must fully support our military forces engaged in combat. To the maximum extent possible, our U.S. military forces must continue to be comprised of volunteer professionals. The U.S. media needs to support U.S. military forces engaged in combat and responsibly present fair and balanced news reports to the American people and world community. The U.S. defense industry needs to continue to responsibly provide U.S. military forces with the most cost-effective and technologically advanced weapons and weapon systems in the world. Finally, our U.S. military forces must continue to be the best trained, best equipped and most highly motivated military forces in the world.

I have gone full circle. I started out to tell the Nimrod story. I hope I have done some justice to the Nimrods who flew A-26 missions in Steel Tiger and Barrel Roll in Laos, and in adjacent areas in North and South Vietnam, from 1966 to 1969. The Nimrods were one of the most unique and effective combat units in American military history. The grueling non-stop combat flight schedule began to take its toll in 1969 when spare parts became scarcer and maintenance became more challenging. According to Nolan Schmidt, an Air Force captain and an A-26 navigator/co-pilot when A-26 flight operations ended at NKP in November 1969, the A-26s began taking more AAA hits and SA7 surface-to-air missiles started appearing along the Trail. More recently, Colonel Nolan Schmidt (USAF-Retired) informed me that the "Wings" series on the History Channel summed up the end of A-26 combat operations by stating "…it wasn't that the Invader wasn't wanted, it was just that there were so few left to use…no other combat aircraft had been used to the last like that." The A-26 saw extensive combat service in three wars: World War II, the Korean War, and finally, the Vietnam War. Few combat aircraft have seen combat service in three wars. Actually, the Air Force explored a re-start of the A-26 production line, but the Air Force was becoming more committed to an all-jet fleet, and the A-10 Warthog jet attack aircraft became the obvious follow-on aircraft to the A-26 Counter Invader. B-57s and C-130 Gunships continued nighttime combat operations over the Trail for a time after A-26 operations concluded in 1969. In any event, I wanted to pass the Nimrod story along to my family, capture the story for the Nimrods and U.S. Air Force history, and make the Nimrod story available for anyone who might be interested. Along the way, I realize that I tried to reach a better understanding of the Vietnam War and the role of the Nimrods in that war. In the process of researching and writing this book I believe I have gained a much better understanding of the reasons the United States entered the war, and the reasons our national leaders were so hesitant to unleash full U.S. military power in a military strategy designed to win a military victory. Having done so, I am even more proud of the courage and effectiveness of the Nimrod A-26 crews in the Vietnam War. The Nimrod story, and the lessons learned in the Vietnam War, must not be forgotten.

CHAPTER 15: LESSONS LEARNED: CURRENT GLOBAL WAR ON TERROR

As I start writing this chapter, the date is January 5, 2007, exactly sixty-two years since my father was killed in combat in the Battle of the Bulge on January 5, 1945. I always feel a very heavy heart and a great sense of loss every time January 5 rolls around again on the calendar. I was not quite three years old when my father was killed in action. I only remember seeing my father one time, and that is when he was waving goodbye to us from the end of the last car of a train departing a train station near our hometown in West Virginia. He was in his Army uniform, he had a broad smile, and he waved to us until the train moved out of sight. The train cars were painted a dark green. The train was pulled by a steam engine and the steam and smoke engulfed the train as it departed. The noise from the train engine and the train cars moving on the track was deafening. For many years I thought the sight of my father waving goodbye to us may have only been a dream, but as I grew older my mother confirmed that my father's last farewell to us occurred exactly as I remember it. It's very difficult for me to imagine the hardship and horror that my father and his Army combat unit experienced in the winter of 1944-45, or the shock and emotional pain experienced by my mother when she learned of his death. My mother was left with three small children to raise by herself. According to a letter to my mother from Sergeant Bruce Powell, dated June 26, 1945 (after Sgt. Powell returned to the States), my father was killed approximately two miles east of Bastogne during a German counterattack. My father and Sergeant Powell shared the same foxhole while fighting the German soldiers in extreme cold and heavy snow conditions. The night before my father was killed, he wounded a German soldier and took him captive. Because of the loss of my father, and because of my personal combat experience with the Nimrods in the Vietnam War, the trauma and brutal reality of war are real to me. I would never advocate that the United States wage war without great justification.

Also, as I start to write this chapter, the United States is engaged in a Global War on Terror initiated on September 11, 2001, when al Qaeda Islamic extremists hijacked four commercial airliners and flew them into the World Trade Center twin tower buildings in New York City, and into the side of the Pentagon in Washington, D.C. No American living on September 11, 2001, will ever forget the shock and absolute disbelief experienced while watching live TV news coverage of the collapse of the two airliner-damaged World Trade Center buildings, and the smoke and fire pouring out of the collapsed southwest side of the Pentagon immediately after impact of that hijacked airliner. Incredibly courageous passengers caused the fourth hijacked airliner to crash in a field in Pennsylvania as the hijackers attempted to reach Washington, D.C. for another suicide crash that probably targeted the White House, the Capitol building, or perhaps another impact with the Pentagon. Approximately 3000 Americans lost their lives that day due to those unprovoked evil attacks masterminded by Osama bin Laden and his al Qaeda terrorist network. The American people and the civilized world community were stunned and outraged by the attacks. A video clip showed Osama bin Laden smiling as he learned of the devastation caused by his al Qaeda suicide hijackers. The response of President George W. Bush and Congress was to authorize American armed forces to attack the al Qaeda training camps in Afghanistan and remove the Taliban from power, and to conduct an invasion of Iraq and remove Saddam Hussein from power. Although Osama bin Laden is still at large (presumably hiding in a remote region of Afghanistan or Pakistan, or perhaps dead), the al Qaeda terrorists and the Taliban forces were no match for American and coalition forces. Some military operations are still being conducted in Afghanistan, but the country is relatively secure. Likewise, Saddam Hussein and his regular military forces were quickly defeated in the spring of 2003 by U.S. and British military forces. Saddam Hussein was convicted of war crimes by an Iraqi court and executed by hanging in December 2006.

Although U.S. and British military forces decisively defeated regular Iraqi military forces in the spring of 2003, and despite the democratic election of a new Iraqi government, Iraq remains in turmoil and U.S. and British forces are still fully engaged in supporting the new Iraqi government as it struggles to bring order and security to Iraq. The unexpected high level of death and destruction (particularly in Baghdad) inflicted by anti-American Islamic militants, and violence inflicted on Muslims by Muslims (Shiite and Sunni sectarian reprisal attacks on each other), continued unabated throughout 2006. As a result, many Americans are calling for the U.S. to pull out of Iraq, and the Bush administration found itself confronted with multiple challenges in the Middle East. A bipartisan Iraq Study Group released its written report in late 2006 and President Bush continues weighing policy and strategy change options in the Iraq War. All of these events since the 9/11 attacks have led to a major foreign policy challenge for the Bush administration, and for global uneasiness in general. We are living at the crossroads of a new world order. Before discussing the options facing the Bush administration and the world community, a brief discussion of U.S. foreign and military policy is warranted.

a. National Foreign Policy Legacy: Walk Softly but Carry A Big Stick

I believe it is fair to say that the national foreign policy legacy of the United States has centered on President Teddy Roosevelt's concept of "Walk Softly but Carry a Big Stick." We have never had a foreign policy of colonization, empire building, unjustly conquering other nations with military might, or unjustly seizing the land or wealth of other nations by military force. We have a foreign policy legacy of being a responsible nation interested in securing and preserving our country and our way of life, of expanding diplomatic and economic opportunities with other countries, and of opposing dictators and tyrants who abuse and murder their own people and attack or threaten the rest of the world. The President is the chief architect of U.S. foreign policy.

Each President recites the following oath, in accordance with Article II, Section I of the U.S. Constitution:

"I do solemnly swear (or affirm) that I will faithfully execute the office of President of the United States, and will to the best of my ability, preserve, protect and defend the Constitution of the United States."

The U.S. State Department has primary responsibility for assisting the President with the formulation and execution of foreign policy:

"The Department of State is the lead U.S. foreign affairs agency. It advances U.S. objectives and interests in shaping a freer, more secure, and more prosperous world through formulating, representing, and implementing the President's foreign policies. The Secretary of State, the ranking member of the Cabinet and fourth in line of presidential succession, is the President's principal adviser on foreign policy and the person chiefly responsible for U.S. representation abroad." [see www.state.gov]

Further, the core mission responsibilities of the State Department include:

"-- Ensure national security by building and maintaining alliances and defusing and preventing crises;

-- Advance the economic interests of the American people by promoting free trade and assisting American businesses;

-- Promote democratic values and respect for human rights; and

-- Provide protection and services to Americans abroad and control access to the United States." [see www.state.gov]

The Department of Defense is the military component of U.S. foreign policy. The President is the Commander-in-Chief of all U.S. military forces. The Secretary of Defense is the top civilian leader of the Department of Defense.

"The Secretary of Defense is the principal defense policy adviser to the President and is responsible for the formulation of general defense policy and policy related to all matters of direct concern to the Department of Defense, and for the execution of approved policy. Under the direction of the President, the Secretary exercises authority, direction and control over the Department of Defense. The Secretary of Defense is a member of the President's Cabinet and of the National Security Council." [see www.defenselink.mil/osd]

Primarily due to major setbacks and challenges in the Iraq War, and gains by the Democratic Party in the House and Senate in the 2006 elections (Democrats replaced Republicans as the majority party in both the House and Senate), Donald Rumsfeld was replaced by Robert Gates as Secretary of Defense. Also due to the perceived deteriorating situation in Iraq (particularly increasing violence in Baghdad), a bipartisan Iraq Study Group was constituted at the urging of several members of Congress, in conjunction with agreement from the White House. The Iraq Study Group was co-chaired by former Secretary of State James A. Baker, III and former Congressman Lee H. Hamilton, and also included the following distinguished Americans in the ten-person group: Robert M. Gates, Vernon E. Jordan, Jr., Edwin Meese III, Sandra Day O'Connor, Leon E. Panetta, William J. Perry, Charles S. Robb, and Alan K. Simpson (5 Republicans and 5 Democrats). Their final report, *The Iraq Study Group Report: The Way Forward – A New Approach*[4], was released to Congress, the White House, and the public on December 6, 2006. The *Iraq Study Group Report* may be purchased at bookstores and is available online at www.usip.org. The main findings and recommendations of that report deserve serious consideration by all Americans.

b. The Iraq Study Group Report

In an introductory letter in the *Iraq Study Group Report* (hereafter, "*Iraq Report*") from James Baker and Lee Hamilton, the co-chairs state that no one can guarantee that any course of action in Iraq at this point will stop sectarian warfare and growing violence, and warn that if current trends continue, the potential consequences could be severe. The co-chairs also emphasized:

"What we recommend in this report demands a tremendous amount of political will and cooperation by the executive and legislative

---

[4] *The Iraq Study Group Report,* James A. Baker III, and Lee H. Hamilton, Co-Chairs, Vintage Books, 2006.

branches of the U.S. government. It demands skillful implementation. It demands unity of effort by government agencies. And its success depends on the unity of the American people in a time of political polarization. Americans can and must enjoy the right of robust debate within a democracy. Yet U.S. foreign policy is doomed to failure—as is any course of action in Iraq—if it is not supported by a broad, sustained consensus. The aim of our report is to move our country toward such a consensus." [*Iraq Report*, page *x*]

In an initial overall assessment, the *Iraq Report* states:

"Iraq is vital to regional and even global stability, and is critical to U.S. interests. It runs along the sectarian fault lines of Shia [also known as Shiite or Shi'ite] and Sunni Islam, and of Kurdish and Arab populations. It has the world's second-largest known oil reserves. It is now a base of operations for international terrorism, including al Qaeda." [*Iraq Report*, p. 1]

Following a detailed assessment of the current situation in Iraq pertaining to security, politics, economics and international support, and a discussion of the consequences of continued decline in Iraq, the Iraq Study Group proceeded to consider, but reject, the following alternative courses of action in Iraq:

1. Precipitate Withdrawal
2. Staying the Course (meaning continuation of present course)
3. More Troops for Iraq
4. Devolution to Three Regions (Sunni, Shia and Kurdish) [*Iraq Report*, pp. 37-39]

The Iraq Study Group stated, "We agree with the goal of U.S. policy in Iraq, as stated by the President: an Iraq that can 'govern itself, sustain itself, and defend itself.'" (*Iraq Report*, p. 40) However, the Iraq Study Group stated that changes in course must be made, both inside and outside Iraq, in order to achieve that goal.

"Externally, the United States should immediately begin to employ all elements of American power to construct a regional mechanism that can support, rather than retard, progress in Iraq. Internally, the Iraqi government must take the steps required to achieve national reconciliation, reduce violence, and improve the daily lives of Iraqis."

[*Iraq Report*, p. 41]

In all, the Iraq Study Group made seventy-nine specific recommendations for actions to be taken in Iraq, the United States, and the region. The *Iraq Study Group Report* should be read by all Americans. The Executive Summary points out that "[t]he situation in Iraq is grave and deteriorating," and states that the Iraq Study Group's "most important recommendations call for new and enhanced diplomatic and political efforts in Iraq and the region, and a change in the primary mission of U.S. forces in Iraq that will enable the United States to move its combat forces out of Iraq responsibly." (*Iraq Report*, p. xiii) The Study Group reported that the violence in Iraq is fed by the Sunni Arab insurgency, Shiite militias and death squads, al Qaeda, and widespread criminality. The Iraq Study Group recommends that the United States immediately launch a new diplomatic offensive to build an international consensus for stability in Iraq and the region: this diplomatic effort should include every country that has an interest in avoiding a chaotic Iraq, including all of Iraq's neighbors. With respect to the destabilizing roles being played by Iran and Syria, the Study Group stated that:

"Iran should stem the flow of arms and training to Iraq, respect Iraq's sovereignty, and territorial integrity, and use its influence over Iraqi Shia groups to encourage national reconciliation. The issue of Iran's nuclear programs should continue to be dealt with by the five permanent members of the United Nations Security Council plus Germany. Syria should control its border with Iraq to stem the flow of funding, insurgents, and terrorists in and out of Iraq." [*Iraq Report*, p. *xv*]

The Iraq Study Group also emphasized the crucial importance of dealing with the Arab-Israeli conflict if peace and stability is to be achieved throughout the Middle East.

"The United States cannot achieve its goals in the Middle East unless it deals directly with the Arab-Israeli conflict and regional instability. There must be a renewed and sustained commitment by the United States to a comprehensive Arab-Israeli peace on all fronts: Lebanon, Syria, and President Bush's June 2002 commitment to a two-state solution for Israel and Palestine. This commitment must include direct talks with, by, and between Israel, Lebanon, Palestinians (those who accept Israel's right to exist), and Syria." [*Iraq Report*, p. *xv*]

With respect to the recommended new internal approach, the Iraq Study Group stated:

"The Iraqi government should accelerate assuming responsibility for Iraqi security by increasing the number and quality of Iraqi Army brigades. While this process is underway, and to facilitate it, the United States should significantly increase the number of U.S. military personnel including combat troops, embedded in and supporting Iraqi Army units. As these actions proceed, U.S. combat forces could begin to move out of Iraq.

"The primary mission of U.S. forces in Iraq should evolve to one of supporting the Iraqi army, which would take over primary responsibility for combat operations. By the first quarter of 2008, subject to unexpected developments in the security situation on the ground, all combat brigades not necessary for force protection could be out of Iraq. At that time, U.S. combat forces in Iraq could be deployed only in units embedded with Iraqi forces, in rapid-reaction and special operations teams, and in training, equipping, advising, force protection, and search and rescue. Intelligence and support efforts would continue. A vital mission of those rapid-reaction and special operations forces would be to undertake strikes against al Qaeda in Iraq." [*Iraq Report*, p. *xvi*]

The Iraq Study Group warned that the United States must not make an open-ended commitment to keep large numbers of troops deployed in Iraq. (*Iraq Report*, p. *xvi*) Significantly, due to the importance of Iraq in our regional security goals and the ongoing fight against al Qaeda, the Iraq Study Group considered proposals to make substantial increases in the numbers of U.S. troops in Iraq (i.e., troop increases in the realm of 100,000 to 200,000). The Study Group decided against recommending troop increases of that magnitude because they did not believe that the needed levels are available for a sustained deployment. **"We could, however, support a short-term redeployment or surge of American combat forces to stabilize Baghdad, or to speed up the training and equipping mission, if the U.S. commander in Iraq determines that such steps would be effective."** (*Iraq Report*, p. 73) (emphasis added)

c. President Bush's Speech Outlining New Strategy in Iraq

On Wednesday night, January 10, 2007, most Americans and many people around the world were riveted to their television sets as President George W. Bush delivered his much-anticipated speech outlining the new U.S. and Iraqi government strategy in Iraq. To set the scene, parts of the speech (e.g., troop surge) had leaked to the press and many Democrats were railing against the speech even before it was delivered by the President. Another developing news story centered on dramatic television and newspaper coverage of ongoing combat action in Somalia involving military forces of Somalia, Ethiopia and the U.S. against al Qaeda terrorists who were driven out of Mogadishu and were on the run in southwest Somalia. The coverage included accounts of U.S. C-130 Gunships attacking al Qaeda leaders and terrorists believed to have been involved in the horrific car bombing attacks against the U.S. embassies in Kenya and Tanzania on August 7, 1998 (257 people killed, another 4000 wounded). Just before the television coverage of President's Bush's speech was to begin, I was very interested in what the President's appearance and body language might tell us. No doubt, so were many other people in America and around the world. As the television camera image of the President first appeared on the screen, my impression was that the President was calm and determined, but that he was shouldering an enormous—almost overwhelming—burden with respect to his responsibilities in Iraq and the War on Terror. Nonetheless, he forcefully and clearly delivered the speech[5] during the allotted half-hour time frame. During the speech, the President made the following major points:

1. The War in Iraq will determine the direction of the global War on Terror and the safety of Americans at home.
2. The election of 2005, in which twelve million Iraqi's cast their ballots, was a stunning achievement.
3. The level of violence and murder by al Qaeda and Sunni insurgents since the elections was unexpected.
4. That level of violence, plus the al Qaeda bombing of the Golden

---

[5] The text of the speech appears at www.cnn.com/2007/POLITICS.

Mosque of Samarra, provoked retaliation by Shia militants and death squads that led to current unrelenting sectarian violence.

5. The current situation in Iraq is unacceptable to Americans.
6. Bush takes responsibility for mistakes that have been made.
7. Bush recognizes that we need to change our strategy in Iraq.
8. Bush has consulted with his national security team, military commanders, diplomats, members of Congress from both parties, our allies abroad and outside experts.
9. The recommendations of the Iraq Study Group were carefully considered.
10. Everyone agrees that failure in Iraq would be a disaster for the United States.
11. The most urgent priority for success in Iraq is security, especially in Baghdad.
12. Bush has committed more than 21,500 additional troops to Iraq to support the elected Iraqi government and its military forces (some 16,500 additional troops in Baghdad, and 4000 more in Anbar Province west of Baghdad to combat al Qaeda forces).
13. New strategy and added force levels will enable troops to hold areas of Baghdad that are cleared, and Iraqi and American forces will have the green light to enter and secure all neighborhoods in Baghdad.
14. Bush has made it clear to Prime Minister Maliki and Iraq's other leaders that America's commitment is not open-ended.
15. Most of Iraq's Sunni and Shia population want to live together in peace, and reducing the level of violence in Baghdad will make reconciliation possible.
16. A successful strategy for Iraq goes beyond military operations.
17. Iraq will pass legislation to share oil revenues among all Iraqis.
18. The Iraqi government will spend $10 billion of its own money on reconstruction and infrastructure projects that will create new jobs.
19. In keeping with the recommendations of the Iraq Study Group, we will increase the embedding of American advisers in Iraqi army units, and partner a coalition brigade with every Iraqi

army division.

20. We will help the Iraqis build a larger and better-equipped army, and we will accelerate the training of Iraqi forces, which remains the essential U.S. security mission in Iraq.

21. We will give our commanders and civilians greater flexibility to spend funds for economic assistance.

22. We will interrupt the flow of support to terrorists and insurgents from Iran and Syria, and we will seek out and destroy the networks providing advanced weaponry and training to our enemies in Iraq.

23. We will work with other countries to prevent Iran from gaining nuclear weapons and dominating the region.

24. We will use America's full diplomatic resources to rally support for Iraq from nations throughout the Middle East, including Saudi Arabia, Egypt, Jordan, and the Gulf states.

25. **The challenge playing out across the broader Middle East is more than a military conflict. It is the decisive ideological struggle of our time.** (emphasis added)

26. "Let me [Bush] be clear: The terrorists and insurgents in Iraq are without conscience, and the year ahead will be bloody and violent."

27. Bush believes the new strategy will bring us closer to success.

28. Acting on the good advice of Senator Joe Lieberman and other key members of Congress, we will form a new, bipartisan working group that will help us come together across party lines to win the war on terror.

29. **In these dangerous times, the U.S. is blessed to have extraordinary and selfless men and women serving in our military forces.** (emphasis added)

30. **The year ahead will demand more patience, sacrifice, and resolve.** (emphasis added)

31. We can and we will prevail.

d. Personal Reaction to President Bush's Speech and the War on Terror

Thank God that I am a citizen of the United States of America, and through freedom of speech I have the right to express my opinion. First, I strongly believe that this is a crucial turning point in history, and that all Americans need to come together and support the President and our military personnel as we fight to achieve success in this War on Terror. As I watched President Bush's speech on television, it appeared that the weight of the world's burdens rested squarely on his shoulders. I tried to understand the expression in his eyes and any signals that his body language might produce. His eyes were shining brightly and they stared straight ahead. As he spoke, I was reminded of the war weariness that showed in President Lyndon Johnson's face as he coped with the unrelenting challenges of the Vietnam War. Neither President wanted to be a wartime President, but world events forced each President to lead the nation in unpopular wars.

Many critics, both in America and in Europe, would like to paint President Bush as a bungling warmonger who deserves all the grief he is reaping in Iraq. With all due respect, I **strongly** disagree with those critics. President Bush did not provoke the reprehensible al Qaeda attacks on New York and Washington, D.C. on September 11, 2001. Immediately after the attacks all Americans expected, even demanded, that President Bush lead a decisive counterattack on the terrorists. I have never seen such a wave of patriotism sweep across America as I saw in the immediate aftermath of the 9/11 attacks. American flags were waving everywhere you looked, from cars on our highways to homes in our neighborhoods. President Bush rightly believed he had a duty under the Constitution, and a mandate from the American people, to initiate a global counterattack against terrorism. Moreover, President Bush and his security team did not act in a vacuum. They helped form a Global Coalition Against Terrorism and acted in good faith to enlist the active support of the United Nations, the North Atlantic Treaty Organization(NATO), and allies in the Middle East and around the world. However, when the dust settled, the United States and the United Kingdom were left with primary responsibility for confronting the terrorists based in the Middle East. President Bush and Britain's former Prime Minister Tony Blair have been strong allies in the War on Terror.

With Congress' authorization, President Bush led us into a justified war in Afghanistan because the al Qaeda terrorists who unmercifully attacked us on September 11, 2001, were allowed to establish extensive terrorist training camps in Afghanistan by the ruling oppressive Taliban (Sunni Islamic fundamentalist) regime. Coalition forces initiated combat operations in Afghanistan on October 7, 2001, and although the conflict is still ongoing, the Taliban has been removed from control of the government, and al Qaeda terrorists (including Osama bin Laden) have been killed or driven into remote mountains along the Afghanistan and Pakistan border. The first waves of attacks in Afghanistan were carried out solely by American and British forces. Thanks in large part to the substantial follow-on involvement of NATO nations (principally including the United Kingdom, Canada, Australia, Denmark, France, Germany, Italy, Netherlands, and Norway) in combat operations in Afghanistan, and the heavy involvement of Afghan Northern Alliance fighters on the coalition side, military operations in Afghanistan have been a success. True, there are still some ongoing operations against the Taliban and al Qaeda terrorists in Afghanistan, but coalition and NATO forces appear to be winning that war. The successes in Afghanistan cry out for more media coverage in America and the world community.

> "In good news, the capital city of Kabul remained secure and the elected government of U.S.-backed President Hamid Karzai was still in power. Around the country, more than 5 million children attended school; 25% of them were girls, who were denied schooling by the Taliban. The size of the country's economy has tripled in the last five years. Support from NATO countries remains solid: there's a consensus in Europe that Afghanistan isn't Iraq; the war there is considered both legal and necessary to keep the nation from reverting to being a safe haven for the Taliban and al-Qaeda." [**TIME:** 2006 The Year in Review]

Also, with Congress' authorization, President Bush led us into a justified war in Iraq in 2003 because militant dictator Saddam Hussein was believed by the intelligence community to possess Weapons of Mass Destruction (WMD) (e.g., chemical, biological and possibly nuclear weapons), because of Hussein's probable ties to al Qaeda and other terrorist organizations, because of Hussein's flagrant violation of U.N. resolutions concerning weapons inspection in Iraq, and because of Hussein's violent history (e.g., Kuwait invasion in 1990, Iraq-Iran War from 1980-1988, and Saddam's violent repression of his own people in Iraq throughout his presidency). (See generally, http://usinfo.state.gov/products/pubs/iraq/homepage.) Hussein's efforts to acquire nuclear weapons had suffered a major setback due to successful Israeli airstrikes on an Iraqi nuclear facility in 1981. Hussein launched chemical attacks against forty Kurdish villages and thousands of innocent civilians in 1987-88. On March 16, 1988, more than 5000 civilians (men, women and children) died horrific deaths as a result of Iraqi chemical attacks on the Kurdish city of Halabja located 150 miles northeast of Baghdad. Documented Iraqi chemical attacks killed more than 30,000 Kurds within Iraq as a result of Hussein's Kurdish population extermination campaign.[6] Even though U.S. forces didn't find the level of WMDs in Iraq that they expected to find, that does not mean that the WMDs were never there. Clearly, Hussein used chemical weapons against the Kurds. Not only was Saddam Hussein one of the most brutal dictators in world history, he was also a master of deception. President William Clinton was convinced that Hussein had WMDs: "[I]t is incontestable that on the day I left office there were unaccounted-for-stocks of biological and chemical weapons." (President Clinton statement, CNN interview, July 2003) See also, *Saddam's Secrets*[7], published in 2006 and available for purchase at Amazon.com, a book written by former Iraqi General Georges Sada (a citizen of Iraq and an Assyrian Christian who values the truth), in which Sada confirms that Hussein had extensive stocks of WMDs (particularly chemical and biological weapons) before the American invasion, and that fifty-six plane loads of the WMDs were secretly flown to Syria shortly before the outbreak of the Iraq War in 2003 (see *Saddam's Secrets*, pages 250-261). Hussein also used large commercial trucks to transport the WMDs to Syria. Sada stated

---

[6] See http://usinfo.state.gov/products/pubs/iraq/homepage

[7] Sada, Georges, with Jim Nelson Black, *Saddam's Secrets,* Integrity Publishers, 2006.

that Hussein planned to order chemical airstrikes against Israel, but Sada talked him out of it because of the likelihood that Israel would have counterattacked with nuclear weapons. Hussein also decided against attacking Israel and Saudi Arabia because U.S. and coalition forces launched Gulf War I on January 17, 1991, and Saddam had his hands full retreating from Kuwait and reacting to coalition attacks on Iraqi military targets (see *Saddam's Secrets*, pages 128-173). Sada believes that Saddam Hussein ordered the use of chemical weapons in the murder of some 195,000 Kurds (see *Saddam's Secrets*, page 189), and that Saddam is responsible for the deaths of an estimated 200,000 to 300,000 Iraqis who Saddam believed opposed him (see *Saddam's Secrets*, page 199).

For the reasons stated above, the Iraq War began on March 20, 2003, with the preemptive invasion of Iraq by U.S. and U.K. forces. Approximately forty other nations joined coalition efforts by providing equipment, services, security and special forces. As extensively documented in live television broadcasts (transmitted by TV journalists embedded with American troops), U.S. and coalition forces quickly overwhelmed and defeated Hussein's regular military forces, and on May 1, 2003, President Bush declared "Mission Accomplished" in a speech aboard an aircraft carrier returning from the Persian Gulf. However, the post-invasion environment (Sunni insurgency, and sectarian and terrorist violence), particularly in Baghdad and the Anbar Province west of Baghdad, has proved to be a major threat to the elected Iraqi government and the initial coalition military victory. In response, President Bush and Iraqi Prime Minister Nouri al-Maliki have agreed to implement a new strategy in Iraq to "clear and hold" districts in Baghdad, and to defeat terrorists in Anbar Province. The new strategy was outlined in President Bush's televised speech on January 10, 2007.

e. Application of Lessons Learned to Iraq War and War on Terror

The lessons learned by Americans in past wars, particularly World War II and the Vietnam War, cry out for application to the War on Terror. There are important distinctions in world conditions during each of those periods, but there are valuable lessons learned that need to be applied to the War on Terror.

- **Americans need to be united**. Americans, and indeed the larger free world, need to be united in confronting and defeating militant Islamic terrorists and ruthless dictators (regardless of ideology) who seek to destroy the United States and the civilized international community. After the ruthless Japanese surprise attack on U.S. naval forces at Pearl Harbor on December 7, 1941, Americans were outraged and the U.S. was thrust into World War II against Japanese leaders who sought to forge an empire in the Pacific, and against Hitler's Nazis who sought to conquer and dominate Europe and the world. The American public was justifiably outraged and united in fighting and winning World War II. During World War II, the entire country mobilized and supported—through military service, industrial transformation, media and Hollywood war coverage, and political and diplomatic initiatives—the policies and strategies of President Roosevelt and President Truman as they led the U.S. war effort. On September 11, 2001, Osama bin Laden's al Qaeda terrorist organization attacked the World Trade Center buildings in New York, and the Pentagon in Washington, D.C.—an unprovoked attack at least as horrendous as the attack on Pearl Harbor on December 7, 1941—resulting in the deaths of more than 3000 civilian men, women and children. Most of those innocent victims were American citizens, but many were citizens of other countries. We could not be more justified in confronting and defeating international criminal terrorists who have attacked us, but to be successful, we must remain united. As time went on in the Vietnam War, the country became less and less united, greatly contributing to our withdrawal and the fall of the South Vietnamese government. This is not a time to play partisan politics, this is a time to unite in the national interest and win the War on Terror. Unfortunately, as we approach the presidential campaigns in America in 2007 and 2008, the Democratic Party has chosen to make the Wars in Iraq and Afghanistan, and the War on Terror, political issues that they believe will win them the White House in 2008. In the process, they have orchestrated a non-binding House and

Senate Resolution calling for the withdrawal of U.S. troops from Iraq by 2008, and passed legislation tying continued funding of the troops to a troop withdrawal date in 2008 (plus "pork" provisions for Democratic districts). President Bush vetoed that ill-advised legislation. Democrats and the Congress could not be more wrong and short-sighted, unless of course, they want to do everything within their power to embolden the enemy and destroy the morale of our U.S. troops who are fighting to win in a situation equal to—or even worse—than the situation faced by U.S. troops in the Vietnam War. As our troops learned in World War II, Korea, and Vietnam—and are learning once again in Iraq and Afghanistan—the world is full of tyrants and terrorists, and the only way to protect and preserve the way of life of the United States of America is by finding the moral strength to fight and defeat those tyrants and terrorists. Congressional funding of U.S. troops engaged in combat should not be a political issue. It is and should be a national defense and military issue. All Americans, regardless of political party, should expect and demand that the United States Government provide for the common defense. Clearly, tyrants and terrorists also present the world and the United States with moral and religious issues that cannot be ignored. If Senator Harry Reid (D-Nevada) and Speaker Nancy Pelosi (D-California) have their way, U.S. troops will be withdrawn from Iraq by election time in 2008. If that happens, Democratic supporters and much of the West will feel much better for a short time. What will they do when the U.S. and the West continue to suffer radical Islamic attacks on par with, or even more horrific than, the attacks on 9/11? How will they prevent the proliferation of nuclear weapons and other Weapons of Mass Destruction? What is the Democratic plan? To succeed, we must be united, and we must have a plan.

- **Americans need to be patient.** Americans have many admirable qualities. Patience is not one of them. However, we need to recognize—when the stakes are high enough—that we need to marshal whatever patience is required in order to defeat an enemy that is intent, and immensely patient, on the destruction of America. Americans and our allies need to recognize that this is a period in history where the stakes pertaining to international terrorists and rogue dictators are very high. Osama bin Laden and the international terrorist network want nothing less than the death of all Americans, and the defeat and destruction of America. We were patient in World War II and we won the war. We lost our patience and will power in the Vietnam War, we pulled out U.S. military forces, and the predictable result was a communist military takeover of South Vietnam. We have already won the War in Iraq and we are fighting to preserve that victory and win the peace. American citizens and politicians need to patiently support U.S. military commanders and U.S. troops as they bring security to Iraq. President Bush has repeatedly warned the American public that the War on Terror will be a long struggle. Significantly, Gordon Brown, the low-key Scotsman and new British Prime Minister succeeding Tony Blair, stated in late July 2007 that: "The United States and Britain are engaged in a generation-long battle against al Qaeda inspired terrorism and Britain absolutely shares President Bush's philosophy on the war on terror."[8] No matter how galling and unpopular it may be, Americans need to understand that success in the War on Terror may take a generation or more to achieve.

- **Americans need to support our military forces.** It seems axiomatic that Americans need to support our military men and women engaged in combat in a time of war. That is clearly what happened in World War II, but Americans started losing sight of that basic concept during the Vietnam War. There was nothing more disheartening to American military personnel (who gave "their all" in Vietnam) than to return home to the United States after a combat tour in the Vietnam War and be ignored or openly despised **by citizens of the United States of**

---

[8] www.cnn.com/2007/07/30/POLITICS/bush.brown/index.html

America! I experienced that distasteful phenomenon in 1968 after completing my combat tour in the Vietnam War and returning home to the United States. Fortunately, that has not happened so far in the War on Terror. Almost everyone agrees that our military men and women have fought bravely and very effectively in Afghanistan and Iraq. At this point in time, we have lost more than 3000 brave American military men and women in the War on Terror, including combat operations in Iraq and Afghanistan. Personally, I am extremely proud of the courage and professionalism that our U.S. military forces have demonstrated in unusually difficult combat conditions (deserts, mountains and urban jungles). Despite monumental challenges, their morale remains high and they are convinced they can win in Iraq and Afghanistan. Their courage and determination to win reminds me of the Nimrod spirit that I experienced with the 609th Special Operations Squadron during the Vietnam War. As the war effort intensifies in Iraq, we must do everything we can do as Americans to demonstrate our unqualified support for our American troops on the battlefield, and for their family members back home. Some are returning for second and third tours. The Army, Air Force, Navy and Marine Corps active duty forces are joined by their counterparts from Guard and Reserve units. **They are all volunteers!!!** They deserve the best equipment and budget support that Congress can provide, and they deserve the heartfelt gratitude of all American citizens. I served a full career with the U.S. Air Force, and a secondary career with Lockheed Martin Corporation developing and manufacturing F-22 and C-130J aircraft, and I want to go on record right here to say **thank you** to all of our brave men and women who are fighting this War on Terror. I also want to go on record and ask **all** American citizens, and **all** members of Congress, to thank our American troops, and their families, for their selfless, patriotic service to our country. You cannot believe how much a simple "thank you" means to our troops and their families.

- **Americans need to support President Bush and successors.**

In the days and weeks immediately following the 9/11 attacks, the great majority of Americans heavily supported President George W. Bush as he comforted the families of the victims, and as he prepared the country for what he called the long War on Terror. We still supported him as Commander-in-Chief as he ordered the invasions of Afghanistan and Iraq. Americans were happy to support President Bush as long as our military efforts were successful in Afghanistan and Iraq, but now that we have run into some real challenges in Iraq, many Americans now want to bash Bush and cut-and-run. Americans need to recognize that President Bush needs and deserves our long-term support. He is exactly the type of leader we need during this period of crisis. He is a person of high moral and religious convictions, he is tough, and he is determined to seize the initiative from ruthless dictators and terrorists who want to murder us and destroy our way of life. American support for Presidents Roosevelt and Truman never wavered in World War II, and we decisively won that war. American support for Presidents Johnson and Nixon gradually evaporated during the Vietnam War, resulting in a withdrawal of our forces and the defeat of South Vietnam. It's already clear that the War on Terror will extend beyond the end of President George Bush's second term in 2008. The message is clear: Americans must come together and support President Bush, and his successors, if we are to be successful in the War on Terror.

- **The American media needs to support our national interest**. During World War II, the American media (primarily newspapers and radio) overwhelming supported our war efforts against Germany and Japan. Americans, including the media, realized that we were in a struggle for our very existence, and the media responded by broadcasting our military victories and lamenting our losses. During World War II, our fighting military forces had no doubt that the American media, including the Hollywood film industry and film stars, were solidly behind them. Sadly, that was not the case during the Vietnam War. The media (television, newspapers, radio and film) grew progressively anti-American as the war proceeded into the late 1960s. Television news programs emphasized daily "body counts" and combat-related atrocities (more emphasis on a few atrocities committed by Americans than the many atrocities committed by the Viet Cong). Even film "stars" like Jane Fonda had the audacity to sit in a North Vietnamese antiaircraft artillery gun position in Hanoi, while media photographs were taken, and criticize the American war effort while American POWs were being tortured and exploited in nearby Hanoi prisons. The North Vietnamese communists counted heavily on negative American media coverage of the war as they patiently waited for Americans to be persuaded by their own media to withdraw support for American involvement in the war. We cannot afford for that to happen again in the U.S. in the War on Terror. I realize that robust freedom of speech and freedom of the press are two of our most valuable American rights, guaranteed by the U.S. Constitution, but the American media can and should act responsibly and operate in such a way that the national interest is supported, not undermined. Americans recognize when television stations and newspapers "spin" the news, or inject bias in what is supposed to be an objective news program or article. Fortunately, the **Fox News** channel and **CNN** have taken the lead in supporting our national interest and fairly reporting U.S. civil and military success stories, as well as setbacks, in Iraq and Afghanistan. Other U.S. television news programs should follow that lead. Americans want and deserve balanced, factual news reporting that supports U.S. national interests, not the interests of our enemies.

- **American politicians need to support the national interest**. For the most part, American politicians from both parties supported the national interest during World War II. That was not true during the Vietnam War. Toward the end of American involvement in the Vietnam War, more and more politicians used, or attempted to use, difficulties encountered in the Vietnam War for personal political advantage. In the end, Congress withheld appropriated funds for continued involvement in the war, U.S. military forces were withdrawn, and North Vietnam communist leaders reciprocated by violating the cease-fire agreement they had signed and invading and conquering South Vietnam. After all of our sacrifices in the Vietnam War (more than 47,000 Americans killed in action), the North Vietnamese communists, and their Soviet and Chinese communist supporters, achieved a political victory against America in the Vietnam War, followed shortly thereafter by a devious military victory against South Vietnam. Americans must not let our politicians defeat us in the War on Terror. One of the most disgusting political displays Americans have witnessed on television occurred the day after President Bush delivered his nationally televised speech on January 10, 2007, outlining a new strategy in Iraq. The day after the speech, when Americans needed to show the world that America is united in the War on Terror, at least six different Democratic senators running for president in the 2008 elections made highly-partisan attacks on the President and his new strategy. Never mind that the President's new strategy closely tracked the recommendations of the bipartisan Iraq Study Group (including the surge in troop strength), and never mind the crucial national interest in success in Iraq and winning the War on Terror. Those particular Democrats preferred to attempt to promote their own personal self-interest over the interest of the nation as a whole. The new Democratic leaders in Congress went so far as to promote a Congressional non-binding resolution opposing the President's troop surge plan for Iraq. Senator Ted Kennedy of Massachusetts appeared on national TV and called for abandoning our troops in Iraq by cutting off Congressional funding for the war effort while our troops are still engaged in combat in a war that he and Congress authorized!!! If dissenting Democratic and Republican politicians have a different plan for defeating terrorists, they need to communicate that plan to the President and to the American people. Senator Harry Reid (D-Nevada), Senate Majority Leader, even went so far as to publicly say that the War in Iraq is "already lost." If President John Kennedy were alive today, he would be shocked to see what has happened to the Democratic Party in America. President Kennedy was a Democratic leader who showed real courage in confronting America's enemies (e.g., Cuban missile crisis in 1962). I believe it is fair to say that none of the current "leaders" of the Democratic Party would make "honorable mention" in JFK's highly acclaimed book, *Profiles in Courage*. I also believe that American voters will reject politicians who lack courage and who place their self-interest over the national interest.

- **America must renew efforts for international support.** Although President Bush and his national security team obtained the military and diplomatic support of many nations in the War in Afghanistan and the Iraq War, the State Department can never rest in its quest to obtain additional support from the international community in the War on Terror. Beginning with the U.S. Embassy takeover by Iranians in 1979, the U.S. and its citizens have suffered many terrorist attacks at the hands of criminal Islamic militants. However, the long list of heinous terrorist attacks has not been limited to 9/11 and the United States. To list a few, other major terrorist attacks have been carried out in the United Kingdom, Spain, Germany, Austria, Russia, India, Japan, Italy, Greece, Israel, Lebanon, Afghanistan, Pakistan, Iraq, Kuwait, Saudi Arabia, Egypt, Algeria, Kenya, Tanzania, Yemen, Somalia, Indonesia and the Philippines.[9] One of those terrorist incidents involved an attempt by Iraqi intelligence agents to assassinate President George H. W. Bush during a visit to Kuwait on April 14, 1993. Since no country is immune to terrorist attacks, all civilized nations have a common interest in forming alliances to combat terrorism. The Iraq Study Group emphasized that the United States should immediately launch a new diplomatic offensive to build an international consensus for stability in Iraq and the region, and recommended that the diplomatic offensive involve all of Iraq's neighbors, including Syria and

---

[9] For a comprehensive chronological listing of terrorist attacks and incidents spanning 1961-2003, see www.state.gov/r/pa/ho/pubs/fs/5902.htm.

Iran. Obviously, this new diplomatic offensive should include the United Nations and NATO. Although the United Nations lacks military muscle, it does play an important role in world opinion. NATO, on the other hand, is a key organization for both Europe and the United States. NATO does have military muscle. NATO countries are making valuable contributions to improved security and economic progress in Afghanistan. Since NATO could play the same valuable role in Iraq, the United States should make every effort to enlist the support of NATO in the important struggle in Iraq to bring stability and peace to Iraqi citizens. President Nicolas Sarkozy of France, a recently elected pro-American conservative, may be an ally in that effort. Additionally, the U.S. should renew efforts to enlist the support of Middle East allies in the War on Terror. The leaders of the legitimate governments of Saudi Arabia, Egypt, Jordan, Lebanon, Turkey, Pakistan and the Gulf states have much to gain if the region can be stabilized. The influence of those leaders on the leaders of Iran, Syria and the Palestinians is immense. Finally, the United States should continue to do everything within its power to bring about peace between Israel and the Palestinians. Secretary of State Condoleezza Rice aggressively engaged in that crucial effort in early 2007. She met with Palestinian President Mahmoud Abbas (moderate Arab leader), Israeli leaders, and Egyptian President Hosni Mubarak. She called for meetings between Israeli and Palestinian leaders to discuss the creation of an independent Palestinian state, and asked Arab allies to help support the fragile elected government in Iraq. America must continue to pursue every reasonable approach to resolving the Israeli-Arab conflict.

- **America and the West must defeat radical terrorists and control WMDs**. Regardless of what might happen in the future, America and the West must do at least two things to preserve freedom and our way of life. First, we must defeat radical terrorists at home and abroad who attack America and the West and who seek to establish a Muslim Caliphate to rule the world. Second, we must find a way to prevent terrorists and tyrants from gaining access to and a means to use Weapons of Mass Destruction (especially nuclear weapons) against America and the West. Regardless of what political and national security decisions are made regarding the wars in Iraq and Afghanistan, America and the West will still have to deal with radical Islamist terrorists and tyrants, and America and the West will still have to deal with terrorists and tyrants who seek to possess and use nuclear weapons and other forms of WMDs. Every nation has a right to self-defense. America and the West must be united and unrelenting in achieving these two crucial objectives.

CHAPTER 16: THE NEED FOR A NEW VISION THAT CAN BE EMBRACED BY THE ENTIRE WORLD

Since the 9/11 attacks, President George Bush has advanced a vision of combating and defeating tyrants and terrorism, and spreading freedom and democracy around the globe. An overview of America's overall international vision and strategy appears at a White House internet website:

For most of the twentieth century, the world was divided by a great struggle over ideas: destructive totalitarian visions versus freedom and equality.

That great struggle is over. The militant visions of class, nation, and race which promised utopia and delivered misery have been defeated and discredited. America is now threatened less by conquering states than we are by failing ones. We are menaced less by fleets and armies than by catastrophic technologies in the hands of the embittered few. We must defeat these threats to our Nation, allies, and friends.

This is also a time of opportunity for America. We will work to translate this moment of influence into decades of peace, prosperity, and liberty. The U.S. national security strategy will be based on a distinctly American internationalism that reflects the union of our values and our national interests. The aim of this strategy is to help make the world not just safer but better. Our goals on the path to progress are clear: political and economic freedom, peaceful relations with other states, and respect for human dignity.

And this path is not America's alone. It is open to all. To achieve these goals, the United States will:

- champion aspirations for human dignity;

- strengthen alliances to defeat global terrorism and work to prevent attacks against us and our friends;

- work with others to defuse regional conflicts;

- prevent our enemies from threatening us, our allies, and our friends, with weapons of mass destruction;

- ignite a new era of global economic growth through free markets and free trade;

- expand the circle of development by opening societies and building the infrastructure of democracy;

- develop agendas for cooperative action with other main centers of global power; and

- transform America's national security institutions to meet the challenges and opportunities of the twenty-first century.[10]

The need for a new world vision is discussed in *The Pentagon's New Map*[11], a visionary book written by Thomas P. M. Barnett, a senior strategic researcher and professor at the U.S. Naval War College. After receiving a Harvard Ph.D. in political science, Tom Barnett has devoted his career to understanding and explaining how the world works and recommending a global strategy and vision for the U.S. to follow in the twenty-first century. Barnett believes that President Bush and his administration have identified the right basic global vision at this

---

[10] www.whitehouse.gov/nsc/2002/nss1.html
[11] Barnett, Thomas P.M., *The Pentagon's New Map*, Berkley Books, New York, 2004.

critical juncture in world history, and that President Bush has been a bold leader who has taken the correct decisive military action following the 9/11 attacks. However, he believes that the Bush administration needs to make dramatic improvements in refining and communicating the global vision for the entire world to see and understand, and he believes that the Pentagon and the State Department need major mission adjustments to be effective in the post-9/11 era.

An illustration of the Pentagon's new map, appearing in the early pages of *The Pentagon's New Map*, was derived by plotting the sites of major U.S. military operations from 1990-2003. At the risk of oversimplification, what became apparent after plotting all of these points on a world map is that the world is divided into a "Functioning Core" consisting of countries with thriving, integrated economies that enjoy security—for the most part—from hostile aggression from tyrants and terrorists, and a "Non-Integrating Gap," consisting of countries that are disconnected from the thriving global economy mainstream and who suffer from serious security shortfalls at the hands of brutal dictators or terrorists. As you might expect, the "Functioning Core" consists of the United States, Europe, Japan, Canada and Australia; it also includes China, India, South Korea, South Africa, Mexico and some countries in South America. Barnett observes that the U.S. is the primary world military power following the collapse of the Soviet Union and the end of the Cold War. He also observes that the Pentagon needs to accelerate the transformation of the U.S. military into two roles. The first role has to do with creating and maintaining a military strike force that has no equal in the world. The second role has to do with establishing a "System Administrator" military force (i.e., dominant peacekeeping security force) that can take over from the strike force after the initial military victory and provide military security while the country in question transitions into becoming a member of the "Functioning Core" group of nations. Barnett would say that the U.S. military performed the first role superbly in both Afghanistan and Iraq; however, he would say the U.S. has been seriously deficient in performing the "System Administrator" role in Iraq after the initial victory. As a result, the Bush administration has run into hot water as it scrambles to deploy additional troops to Iraq and revise strategy to defeat insurgents and terrorists, defuse sectarian violence, and preserve the initial military victory.

Barnett gives ample credit to other strategic thinkers he has worked with during his career. What their vision boils down to is that they want the U.S. and its allies to pursue a long-term vision that invites every nation and all people to join the global "Functioning Core," thereby expanding global security and global economic opportunity and prosperity for the entire world:

> "America provides the world a security product that is unrivaled, that has made globalization the immense success that it is today for roughly two-thirds of the world's population, and that export will serve as the crucial first ingredient to extending globalization to the remaining third that currently does not enjoy its peace and prosperity. I see the Pentagon as both Leviathan to this world-historical process, and as System Administrator. By Leviathan, I mean America provides the *might* that will eventually outlaw all mass violence in the Gap, and by System Administrator, I mean America must make *right* every security deficit it seeks to fill throughout the Gap. For if we simply engage in drive-by regime change without waging the peace that must follow all such wars, then all our victories will remain forever hollow, and they will necessarily be repeated time and time again. *Desert Storm* was a hollow victory because all it did was beget *Operation Iraqi Freedom*, and that victory will likewise ring hollow until Iraq as a whole is integrated into the global economy and thus safely netted into the Core's collective security." [*The Pentagon's New Map*, p. 310]

Clearly stated, shouldn't America's new vision for the future of all people be the creation of a world where all people are entitled to freedom, democracy, justice, security and economic opportunity? The concepts of life, liberty and the pursuit of happiness are encompassed within the terms, "freedom, democracy, justice, security and economic opportunity,"…so are the concepts of human dignity and freedom of religion. The concept of democracy is important because it empowers each individual to have a vote on who his or her leaders will be, and how basic government issues are resolved. Justice requires that individuals and organizations seeking economic opportunity in the global economy will be required to comply with applicable economic rules and the rule of law. That is a new vision that can be embraced by the entire world. Conservatives and liberals can embrace that new world vision. Democrats and Republicans can embrace that new world vision. In fact, all fair-minded people all across the globe can embrace that new world vision. As Tom Barnett would say, "That is a future worth creating!" The only people who would not want to embrace that new world vision are terrorists, tyrants and criminals. The new world vision articulated above stands out in sharp contrast to the vision of Osama bin Laden, the most noted terrorist of our age.

a. Osama bin Laden's Vision he wants Muslims to Embrace

When the horrific terrorist attacks on America occurred on September 11, 2001, few Americans—and in fact, few people around the world—had ever heard of Osama bin Laden (sometimes spelled Usama Bin Laden). That all changed in the days and weeks following the attacks as a stunned nation tried to come to grips with the magnitude of the tragedy, and tried to understand who was responsible for this atrocity against so many innocent people. In time, a duly constituted 9/11 Commission investigated the tragedy and reported their findings.

> Bin Laden shares Qutb's [Egyptian Muslim extremist] stark view, permitting him and his followers to rationalize even unprovoked mass murder as righteous defense of an embattled faith. Many Americans have wondered, Why do "they" hate us? Some also ask, "What can we do to stop these attacks?"
> Bin Laden and al Qaeda have given answers to both these questions. To the first, they say that America had attacked Islam; America is responsible for all conflicts involving Muslims. Thus Americans are blamed when Israelis fight with Palestinians, when Russians fight with Chechens, when Indians fight with Kashmiri Muslims, and when the Philippine government fights ethnic Muslims in its southern islands. America is also held responsible for the governments of Muslim countries, derided

by al Qaeda as "your agents." Bin Laden has stated flatly, "Our fight against these governments is not separate from our fight against you." These charges found a ready audience among millions of Arabs and Muslims angry at the United States because of issues ranging from Iraq to Palestine to America's support for their countries' repressive rulers.

Bin Laden's grievance with the United States may have started in reaction to specific U.S. policies but it quickly became far deeper. To the second question, what America could do, al Qaeda's answer was that America should abandon the Middle East, convert to Islam, and end the immorality and godlessness of its society and culture: "It is saddening to tell you that you are the worst civilization witnessed by the history of mankind." If the United States did not comply, it would be at war with the Islamic nation, a nation that al Qaeda's leaders said, "desires death more than you desire life."[12]

Incredibly, and almost completely unknown to America and the world community, Osama bin Laden had declared war on America well before September 11, 2001. The 9/11 Commission Report includes the following explanation concerning the foundation of the new terrorism.

"2.1 A DECLARATION OF WAR

In February 1998, the 40-year-old Saudi exile Usama Bin Laden and a fugitive Egyptian physician, Ayman al Zawahiri, arranged from their Afghan headquarters for an Arabic newspaper in London to publish what they termed a fatwa issued in the name of a "World Islamic Front." A fatwa is normally an interpretation of Islamic law by a respected Islamic authority, but neither Bin Laden, Zawahiri, nor the three others who signed this statement were scholars of Islamic law. Claiming that America had declared war against God and

---

[12] 9/11 Commission Report, p. 51; www.gpoaccess.gov/911/pdf/fullreport.pdf

his messenger, they called for the murder of any American, anywhere on earth, as the "individual duty for every Muslim who can do it in any country in which it is possible to do it."

Three months later, when interviewed in Afghanistan by ABC-TV, Bin Laden enlarged on these themes. He claimed it was more important for Muslims to kill Americans than to kill other infidels. "It is far better for anyone to kill a single American soldier than to squander his efforts on other activities," he said. Asked whether he approved of terrorism and of attacks on civilians, he replied: "We believe that the worst thieves in the world today and the worst terrorists are the Americans. Nothing could stop you except perhaps retaliation in kind. We do not have to differentiate between military or civilian. As far as we are concerned, they are all targets."[13]

This brings us to Osama bin Laden's vision for the world.

Bin Laden's Worldview

Despite his claims to universal leadership, Bin Laden offers an extreme view of Islamic history designed to appeal mainly to Arabs and Sunnis. He draws on fundamentalists who blame the eventual destruction of the Caliphate on leaders who abandoned the pure path of religious devotion. He repeatedly calls on his followers to embrace martyrdom since "the walls of oppression and humiliation cannot be demolished except in a rain of bullets." For those yearning for a lost sense of order in an older, more tranquil world, he offers his "Caliphate" as an imagined alternative to today's uncertainty. For others, he offers simplistic conspiracies to explain their world.[14]

Is Osama bin Laden's view a rational view? Did America really declare war against God and his messenger? Did America really do anything to Arabs and Muslims that justified the 9/11 attacks masterminded by Osama bin Laden and his al Qaeda terrorists that killed over 3000 innocent civilians, destroyed the twin towers of the

[13] 9/11 Commission Report, p. 47; www.gpoaccess.gov/911/pdf/fullreport.pdf
[14] 9/11 Commission Report, pp. 50-51; www.gpoaccess.gov/911/pdf/fullreport.pdf

World Trade Center, and heavily damaged the Pentagon? The answer to those questions is a resounding **No** !!!

b. The War within the War: Free World Vision vs. Radical Islamic Vision

Which vision for the future will the world embrace? The vision of the free world emphasizes freedom, democracy, justice, security and economic opportunity. The vision of Osama bin Laden, and his partners in crime, emphasizes death to all who oppose them, martyrdom (death for their own people), and re-establishment of the "Caliphate" to rule the world. Which vision will the people of the Middle East and the rest of the world choose? There is no doubt that the non-Arab and non-Muslim parts of the world will choose, or have already chosen, freedom, democracy, justice, security and economic opportunity. The present war within the war has to do with Osama bin Laden, terrorists and radical Muslim clerics trying to brainwash and intimidate Arabs and Muslims to fight an unjustified and irrational war against the West. The underlying war within the war is a war for the hearts and minds of the people—particularly children and young adults—in the Middle East and around the world. In the long run, it is a more important war than the present war of bullets and bombs. America and the rest of the free world need to recognize this truth and do whatever it takes to communicate this message of competing visions to the Middle East and to the rest of the world. Karen Hughes, the Under Secretary of State for Public Diplomacy and Public Affairs at the State Department, is a communications and public affairs expert who could effectively communicate this message to the world. She needs help from the private sector. All forms of information technology (television, internet, radio, etc.) must be used to reach people in the Middle East and around the world. The terrorist vision of hatred and endless, indiscriminate violence only has appeal to the terrorists who hope to use terrorism to gain power. On January 16, 2007, terrorists used an individual suicide bomber with an explosive vest, and another suicide bomber with a car bomb, to kill seventy students, and wound another 170 students and bystanders, at a university in Baghdad. Taqi al-Moussawi, Dean of the university, said the students belonged to all religions, sects and ethnic groups. The Dean was quoted as saying, "The terrorists want to stop education…those students had nothing to do with politics. They only came to the university to learn." Recently, another Muslim youth was quoted as saying that the radical, Islamic militants have a mental illness. If given a choice, the majority of Arabs and true Muslims—particularly the young—will chose the vision of freedom, democracy, justice, security and economic opportunity. When that happens, good will have triumphed over evil, and people around the world will be free to pursue a life worth living.

CHAPTER 17: THE CONTINUING THREAT OF WEAPONS OF MASS DESTRUCTION (WMD)

Weapons of mass destruction—chemical, biological and nuclear weapons—continue to pose a major threat to the entire world. Chemical weapons (e.g., mustard gas, and nerve agents such as sarin, tabun and VX) were actually used by Saddam Hussein and his regime against the Kurds in northern Iraq in the 1987-88 time frame, killing an estimated 195,000 men, women and children. Thousands more were blinded, maimed, disfigured and permanently disabled. Biological warfare, also known as germ warfare, is the use of any pathogen (bacterium, virus or other disease-causing organism), or toxin found in nature, as a weapon of war. Anthrax is considered one of the most effective agents for biological weapons. A pneumonic anthrax infection starts with ordinary "cold" symptoms and quickly becomes lethal, with a fatality rate that is 80% or higher. Although there have been several incidents involving the suspected use of anthrax since the 9/11 terrorist attacks, apparently few verifiable terrorist attacks using biological weapons have occurred to date. Probably the main reason terrorists have not used chemical and biological weapons more widely is the great difficulty encountered in transporting and using such weapons, and the great risks of death and disease the weapons would pose to the terrorists themselves. The third form of weapons of mass destruction—nuclear weapons—poses the greatest risk of all.

Fortunately, nuclear weapons have not been used in war since the end of World War II. Currently, numerous countries are known to possess nuclear weapons (e.g., U.S., Russia, United Kingdom, France, China, Israel, Pakistan and India). As a former U.S. Air Force B-52 navigator-bombardier in the 1960s, I lived in the chilling Cold War environment that made nuclear war between the U.S. and the former Soviet Union a real possibility. The Cuban Missile Crisis in 1962 came close to triggering a nuclear exchange between the U.S. and the Soviet Union. The crisis began on October 16, 1962, when U.S. reconnaissance data confirming Soviet nuclear missile installations in Cuba were shown to President John F. Kennedy, and ended twelve days later on October 28, 1962, when Soviet premier Nikita Khrushchev announced that the installations would be dismantled. The Cuban Missile Crisis is often regarded as the moment when the Cold War came closest to escalating into a nuclear war. No doubt, the main reason that nations possessing nuclear weapons have not used them against each other is the realization that all participants will probably be destroyed as a result of nuclear war. The concept of Mutually Assured Destruction (MAD) is just as viable today as it was in the Cold War.

The prospect of terrorists or tyrants getting their hands on nuclear weapons is the biggest threat faced by the world today. Most countries that do not have nuclear weapons, with the exception of Iran and North Korea, have opted not to try to obtain them. The United Nations is very active in efforts to stop the proliferation of nuclear weapons. With respect to Iran, Resolution 1737 was passed under Article 41 of the U.N. Charter which allows for economic sanctions, but not the use of military force. It mandates that all U.N. member states "prevent the supply, sale or transfer...of all items, materials, equipment, goods and technology which could contribute to Iran's enrichment-related, reprocessing or heavy water-related activities or to the development of nuclear weapon delivery systems".[15] President Mahmoud Ahmadinejad of Iran continues to maintain that Iran's nuclear program is only intended for peaceful purposes, but it is well known that the uranium enrichment activities being carried out by Iran could be used either for nuclear reactors or, at purer concentrations, for

---

[15] http://news.bbc.co.U.K./1/hi/world/middle_east/4031603.stm

the core of nuclear weapons. President Ahmadinejad's fiery rhetoric denying that the Jewish Holocaust ever took place during World War II, and calling for the destruction of Israel, have unnerved the entire world, including conservatives and reformists in his own country. North Korea, arguably one of the most unstable and most dangerous countries in the world, reportedly conducted its first nuclear weapon test on October 9, 2006. The United Nations is taking the threat seriously, and six nations (North Korea, China, United States, Russia, Japan and South Korea) are actively engaged in talks concerning the crisis.[16] Unexpectedly, Iran's continued pursuit of nuclear capabilities, despite U.N. actions and sanctions to the contrary, has prompted other nations in the Middle East (Saudi Arabia, Egypt, Turkey, Syria, Jordan, Kuwait, Bahrain, Qatar, United Arab Emirates, Oman and Yemen) to announce in 2007 that they are also planning for nuclear power or considering it. The obvious threat to security in the Middle East and the world is that one or more of those countries will pursue development of nuclear power (electricity) for peaceful purposes, and simultaneously pursue secret development of nuclear weapons. This is a foreign affairs crisis of monumental proportions.

Terrorists are probably not going to be able to develop nuclear weapons on their own, but if a country possessing nuclear weapons should ever provide, or be forced to provide, nuclear weapons to a terrorist organization, the world could quickly be pushed to the brink of nuclear disaster. One chilling possibility would be an al Qaeda seizure of nuclear weapons from the government of Pakistan. According to the 9/11 Commission Report, Osama bin Laden made an unsuccessful attempt to obtain nuclear weapons from Sudanese operatives. (9/11 Commission Report, p. 60) Likewise, if Iran or North Korea should acquire or develop nuclear weapons, and a means to deliver them, the world could be coerced into a nuclear confrontation. The *Iraq Study Group Report* recommends, at Recommendation 10, that: "The issue of Iran's nuclear program should continue to be dealt with by the United Nations Security Council and its five permanent members (i.e., the United States, United Kingdom, France, Russia, and China)

[16] http://topics.nytimes.com/top/news/international/countriesandterritories/northkorea/index.html?excamp=GGGNnorthkoreanuclear

plus Germany." If that effort is not successful within a reasonable time frame, Israel may decide that it has no alternative to launching a preemptive strike against the Iranian nuclear facilities (as it did against the Iraqi nuclear facilities in 1981). If that should happen, a world crisis will immediately engulf the world.

CHAPTER 18: CONCLUSION

As I reflect back on my experiences flying combat missions with the Nimrods in the tumultuous Vietnam War era, I feel a deep sense of pride that the Nimrods were a courageous and highly effective fighting force opposing the spread of communism in Southeast Asia. The Nimrods returned to the fight night after night against an enemy determined to kill them and impose communism on the people of South Vietnam, Laos, Cambodia and the entire region. The Nimrods wanted to win and believed they could win. The Nimrods were joined in the fight by many other courageous American military units that wanted to win. Unfortunately, too much of the American media, and too many self-serving politicians, undermined that war effort. Americans were not united at home, they didn't give President Johnson and President Nixon the support they needed, and they didn't exercise the patience needed to win that difficult war. The American military forces were not defeated; they won every significant battle in the war. America did not succeed in that war because political pressure forced the President to sign a cease-fire agreement and withdraw American military forces. Within two years of signing the agreement, North Vietnamese communist leaders violated the cease-fire agreement and sent an invading army of thirty divisions into South Vietnam where they defeated the South Vietnamese military forces and destroyed the South Vietnamese government, ending all dreams of freedom and democracy for the people of South Vietnam.

As I reflect on the 9/11 terrorist attacks and the current world crisis playing out in the Middle East in 2007, I understand why President Bush looked overstressed during his speech to America, and to the world, on January 10, 2007. He knows that America's War on Terror is just, and that this is the time to show strength (not weakness), but he also realizes that war still rages in Iraq (especially in Baghdad), that the Arab-Israeli conflict remains unresolved, and that he needs more support from the international community and from Americans at home. The United Kingdom has been America's staunchest ally in the War on Terror and the War in Iraq. Prime Minister Tony Blair, an incredible visionary leader in his own right, has said repeatedly that the course that America and the U.K. have taken, and continue to take, is exactly the right course of action that must be taken against terrorists and tyrants at this point in history. Tony Blair stepped down as Prime Minister in June 2007, and his successor, Gordon Brown, was immediately faced with attempted terrorist car bombing attacks in central London and at the commercial airport in Glasgow. Obviously, if the democratically elected Iraqi government is to be successful, Prime Minister Maliki and other Iraqi leaders in the Iraqi government must end sectarian violence and help American and U.K. forces defeat the terrorists and insurgents and establish security for all Iraqi citizens.

America's main Arab allies in the Middle East—Saudi Arabia, Egypt, Jordan and the Gulf states—who have the most to lose if Iraq is taken over by terrorist organizations or Iran—continue to sit by on the sidelines as America and the U.K. carry almost the entire war burden. It's past time for the leaders of Saudi Arabia, Egypt, Jordan and the Gulf states to wake up and start providing real support to the allies in the Iraq War. They are making billions of dollars of profit from oil sales in the global marketplace. They need to allocate significant dollar amounts from those profits to the war effort. Clearly, they have the funds to support the U.S. and its allies. They could provide valuable training to Iraqi army and security forces, and they could send peacekeeping forces to Iraq and Afghanistan. They could exert their influence to reign in Iran and Syria as they support terrorists and interfere in the internal affairs of Lebanon and Iraq. And probably most important of all, they could be key facilitators (along with the U.S. and European countries) in bringing about a just resolution of the Israeli-Palestinian stalemate, leading to the dismantling of Hezbollah, Hamas and other terrorist organizations in the Middle East. The rival Hamas and Fatah movements are currently engaged in a bloody power struggle over the Palestinian government, and Arab leaders in the region need to act to stabilize the situation. If they continue to fail to act, they will certainly find themselves in the crosshairs of the terrorists if Iraq should fall to the terrorists or Iran, or if Israeli-Palestinian violence spills over into their countries. It's already clear that Iran plans to use terrorist proxies to destabilize and dominate other countries in the Middle East. In a significant development in July 2007, the U.S. initiated talks with officials from Saudi Arabia, the United Arab Emirates, Kuwait, Qatar, Bahrain and Oman concerning a 10-year multi-billion dollar arms sale package designed to counter Iranian ambitions in the region.[17] Israel and Egypt would continue to receive foreign military assistance support from the United States.

Iranian leaders are pursuing nuclear capabilities and they are providing advanced military missiles, powerful roadside bombs, many different types of IEDs (Improvised Explosive Devices) and other advanced military technology to Hezbollah, Hamas, and to other terrorist organizations and Muslim sects in Iraq and the region. Despite Iran's economic woes, Iran dreams of grandeur in the Middle East and provides $300 million annually to support Hezbollah and Shiite leader Hassan Nasrallah in Lebanon (see **TIME:** 2006 The Year in Review, p. 42). Why would President Mahmoud Ahmadinejad provide $300 million a year to Hezbollah (a terrorist organization within Lebanon that wages war against Israel and threatens to take over the democratically elected government of Lebanon)? Hezbollah and Israeli military forces engaged in warfare in the summer of 2006. In fiery speeches to the Iranian people, Ahmadinejad has declared the Holocaust a "myth," said Israel should be "wiped away," and called the Jewish state "a stain of disgrace...." (**TIME:** 2006 The Year in Review, p. 40) American soldiers under General Dwight D. Eisenhower, who liberated the Nazi concentration camps at the end of World War II, know that the Holocaust was real: they photographed and filmed the horrific death camps to serve as lasting historic proof of unimaginable human suffering and death that took place in those death camps. Why does Ahmadinejad distort history and hate Israel with that level of contempt? Ahmadinejad claimed in an interview with *Time* correspondents that he is a good friend with the U.S., but government-sanctioned street rallies in Tehran and other Iranian cities depict the

---

[17] http://www.cnn.com/2007/POLITICS/07/31/us.mideast.ap/index.html

U.S. and Israel as criminal states. If you look at Ahmadinejad's actions rather than his rhetoric, his preferred friend is Russia, from whom he has recently procured sophisticated antiaircraft missile defense systems, and who he turns to with requests for uranium enrichment technology and mediation assistance with the U.N. and the International Atomic Energy Agency. Iran currently has an estimated eighteen to thirty nuclear facilities, and shows no sign of heeding U.N. Security Council (U.S, U.K., France, China and Russia) proposals to halt uranium enrichment. (**TIME**: 2006 The Year in Review, p. 50)

Never mind that America and the U.K. removed Iran's arch enemy (Saddam Hussein) from power in Iraq. Saddam had brutally waged war against Iran from 1980-1988. But instead of being grateful, Iranian leaders continue to show nothing but contempt for America and the U.K. as they make irresponsible threats against Israel and undermine stability in Iraq. Even more disturbing, Iranian leaders appear determined to obtain nuclear weapons despite U.N. objections. With assistance from Russia, Iran has completed 95% of requirements for nuclear facilities. Iranian leaders claim that they are only pursuing nuclear capabilities for peaceful purposes. But what rational person would trust the Iranian leaders with their rhetoric and threats to wipe Israel off the map?

It is past time for America and the West to recognize that most do not understand their radical Islamic enemies, and that they must do whatever is necessary to understand Islam and the world of Islamic militant extremists who threaten America and the world. It is axiomatic in wartime that it is highly advantageous to understand your enemies in order to defeat your enemies. It is fair to say that most Americans do not understand Islam or Islamic militants who want to destroy America and the West and establish a new world order ruled by Islamic tyrants (the new Caliphate). Almost six years after 9/11, the United States still isn't sure who speaks for Islam. That's understandable, considering that most Muslims in America and the world do not understand who speaks for Islam. The world recognizes that the Pope speaks for the Roman Catholic Church. The Pope has spoken out to the world and condemned terrorism. Who, if anyone, speaks for Islam? It is still an open question whether or not mainstream Islam is compatible with democracy and rights established by the U.S. Constitution and international law. A most disturbing question—why haven't we heard or seen more Islamic clerics speaking out and condemning Islamic militants who murder innocent men, women and children in their terrorist attacks? Although there is disagreement among Muslims in America, some liberal Middle East experts say that we should be asking Muslims and Islamists to clarify exactly what they stand for. In a policy paper, three Carnegie Endowment associates, Amr Hamzawy, Marina Ottaway, and Nathan Brown, call for clarification in six "gray zones": application of *Sharia* law, violence, political pluralism, individual freedoms, minorities, and women's rights. See "Fighting for the Soul of Islam," **U.S. News & World Report**, April 16, 2007, p. 40. We must understand our enemies to defeat our terrorist enemies.

Where do we go from here in defending the U.S. and the West from radical Islamic extremists who want to destroy America and the West? For those who treasure freedom, we cannot follow "leaders" in the Democratic Party in the U.S. that favor short-term political advantage over long-term political reality and security. Senate Majority Leader Senator Harry Reid (D-Nevada) and Speaker Nancy Pelosi (D-California) echo Democratic presidential candidates Hillary Clinton, Barak Obama and John Edwards who want to withdraw troops from Iraq by the end of 2008. The Democrats have not communicated any meaningful plan for dealing with the Wars in Iraq, Afghanistan and the War on Terror to the American people. On April 20, 2007, Senator Reid announced that the war in Iraq is "lost." In response, Senator Mitch McConnell (R-Kentucky) stated, "I can't begin to imagine how our troops in the field, who are risking their lives every day, are going to react when they get back to base and hear that the Democrat leader of the United States Senate has declared the war is lost." In contrast, Rep. David Obey (D-Wisconsin) stated, "Our troops won the war clearly, cleanly and quickly, but now they are stuck in a civil war, and the only solution is a political and diplomatic compromise, and there is no soldier who can get that done."[18] Whether the sectarian and terrorist violence in Iraq amounts to a civil war is a debatable issue; however, it's a fact that U.S. and coalition forces won the initial war against Saddam Hussein and his military forces as early as May 2003. What remains to

---

[18] http://www.cnn.com/2007/POLITICS/04/20/reid.iraq.ap/index.html

be done in Iraq is to preserve that victory and win the peace. We can follow opportunistic, limited vision politicians, withdraw from Iraq, and face a strengthened terrorist movement in the U.S. and around the world, or we can follow the realists, finish the job in Iraq, and defeat terrorists in Afghanistan and the rest of the world. Regardless of which course the U.S. takes, the militant Islamic terrorists are not going to go away until U.S. and coalition forces defeat them. General Georges Sada, who is working for religious and political reconciliation in Iraq, warned the U.S. and the West in *Saddam's Secrets* that appeasement will not work with terrorists, and that overwhelming military force must be applied to defeat the radical Islamic terrorists.

It is past time for the countries of the European Union and NATO to wake up and start providing meaningful military and financial support to America and the U.K. in the War in Iraq, and the larger crisis in the Middle East. NATO is providing meaningful support for the War in Afghanistan. NATO must provide the same support in Iraq while it still has the opportunity. If NATO continues to fail to act in Iraq, European countries will certainly find themselves in the crosshairs of the terrorists if Iraq falls to the terrorists or Iran. European countries are increasingly finding themselves threatened with growing radical Muslim populations. Remember the lesson from appeasement efforts with Hitler immediately before World War II? It did not work. The radical Islamist terrorists of today are at least as determined as Hitler and the radical Nazis in World War II.

In one promising development in late January 2007, international donors meeting in Paris pledged $7.6 billion in aid and loans to raise money for Lebanon's U.S-backed Prime Minister Fuad Saniora and his beleaguered democratically elected government. The conference was hosted by French President Jacques Chirac, and included more than 40 nations and financial institutions that took turns in announcing their contributions. Saudi Foreign Minister Prince Saud al-Faisal pledged $1 billion in development funding, and an additional $100 million grant for the Lebanese government. The U.S. is seeking an additional $770 million in new aid for Lebanon following last summer's Hezbollah-Israeli war. Hezbollah's entrenchment in Lebanon resulted in major damage to Lebanon, and Hezbollah continues to threaten both the Lebanese government and Israel.

America and the U.K. should seek and welcome support, in whatever form, from other countries around the world that enjoy the benefits of the global economy: Japan, China, Russia, India and Brazil come to mind. The voice of the U.N. against terrorists and tyrants needs to be heard. Finally, the American public, the American media, and American politicians (both Republicans and Democrats) need to continue to provide united support to President Bush and U.S. troops as they resolutely press to defeat terrorists and achieve success in Iraq and Afghanistan. If President Bush is not successful in the time remaining in his term, the cancer of terrorism will surely extend beyond his presidency and continue growing in the Middle East and the rest of the world.

In his televised speech on January 10, 2007, President Bush stated that the challenge playing out across the broader Middle East is more than a military conflict, it is the ideological struggle of our time.

"The challenge playing out across the broader Middle East is more than a military conflict. It is the decisive ideological struggle of our time. On one side are those who believe in freedom and moderation. On the other side are extremists who kill the innocent, and have declared their intention to destroy our way of life. In the long run, the most realistic way to protect the American people is to provide a hopeful alternative to the hateful ideology of the enemy - by advancing liberty across a troubled region. It is in the interests of the United States to stand with the brave men and women who are risking their lives to claim their freedom - and to help them as they work to raise up just and hopeful societies across the Middle East."

"From Afghanistan to Lebanon to the Palestinian territories, millions of ordinary people are sick of the violence, and want a future of peace and opportunity for their children. And they are looking at Iraq. They want to know: Will America withdraw and yield the future of that country to the extremists - or will we stand with the Iraqis who have made the choice for freedom?"

"The changes I have outlined tonight are aimed at ensuring

the survival of a young democracy that is fighting for its life in a part of the world of enormous importance to American security. Let me be clear: The terrorists and insurgents in Iraq are without conscience, and they will make the year ahead bloody and violent. Even if our new strategy works exactly as planned, deadly acts of violence will continue - and we must expect more Iraqi and American casualties. The question is whether our new strategy will bring us closer to success. I believe that it will."[19]

As President Bush has stated repeatedly, the War on Terror is not a war on Islam or a war on Muslims. Freedom of religion is one of the basic rights established in the U.S. Constitution. People of all religious beliefs (including Muslims) are permitted to practice their particular religious beliefs in the United States; however, that does not mean that radical Muslims or any other religious sect has the right to subjugate or murder others who do not agree with their religious beliefs. The War on Terror is a war on terrorists, who are nothing more than international criminals who seek power and plunder, and who take sadistic pleasure in the murder, "martyrdom," and physical and mental suffering of all people and all religions around the world. We need for legitimate Muslim clerics to answer the following questions. Are terrorists who murder innocent people true Muslims? Does the Koran (Qur'an) call for, or condone, the murder of non-Muslims? Is Islam a faith of love, or a faith of hate? Why aren't legitimate Islamic clerics and leaders condemning Islamic terrorists who murder innocent people? As to the immediately preceding question, I suspect the answer has to do with fear of becoming victims of terrorists. However, despite the terrorist threats, three legitimate Islamic clerics recently spoke out and condemned radical terrorists (including suicide bombers) who murder civilians and other non-combatants; they uniformly concluded that the Koran (Qur'an) neither calls for, nor condones, the murder of innocent people. One of the Islamic clerics stated that: "Suicide bombing of civilian targets is evil and prohibited under Islamic Law. I would tell suicide bombers intending to attack civilians that they

---

[19] http://www.cnn.com/2007/POLITICS/01/10/bush.transcript/index.html

would be murderers, not martyrs, and that they would go to Hell, not Heaven."[20]

The new Iraq strategy explained by President Bush during his speech on January 10, 2007, does have a real chance of success. It is a new strategy because American soldiers will back up the Iraqi Army, as all of Baghdad's nine districts are included in a new "clear and hold" strategy. None of the terrorists, Muslim militias or insurgents will be off limits. The President is sending an additional 21,500 American soldiers into the battle (17,500 in Baghdad and 4000 in the Anbar Province). The Iraq Study Group expressly acknowledged that a surge of American troops might be required to stabilize Baghdad, or to speed up the training and equipping mission of Iraqi soldiers (see *Iraq Report*, p. 73). Another major reason the new strategy has a real chance for success is that General David Petraeus has been placed in command of all U.S. forces in Iraq. General Petraeus is a genuine heavyweight in military circles. He is a graduate of West Point and Princeton University. He is a Vietnam War veteran. He is also a veteran of the War in Iraq. In an earlier combat tour in Iraq, General Petraeus served in Mosul, in northern Iraq, and he was deeply respected by both American soldiers and Iraqi citizens. Although he is a tireless soldier, he is a leader who sees the big picture. He knows how to identify and reach out to suffering indigenous populations in a chaotic war zone. He understands the importance of defending the defenseless and spending money to improve their lives. Part of the President's new strategy is to empower General Petraeus and other commanders and civil authorities to use their judgment in spending money to improve the lives of the people of Iraq. The Iraqis in Mosul loved him and his style, and in a real display of admiration and gratitude, nicknamed him the new "King David." What greater compliment could a beleaguered Iraqi populace pay to an American Army General Officer? They called him "King David." Based largely upon lessons learned in Vietnam, General Petraeus recently led a complete rewrite of the U.S. Army's Counterinsurgency doctrine. The new doctrine emphasizes patience, the criticality of U.S. public support, the establishment of a legitimate foreign government supported by its people, the training of foreign

[20] http://newsweek.washingtonpost.com/onfaith/projects/muslims.speakout/index.html

security forces, and acknowledges that soldiers and marines should prepare to engage in both combat roles and non-military nation building roles. While President Bush and his security team set the strategy, General Petraeus must be given the latitude to formulate the tactics in Baghdad and the rest of Iraq. The tactics employed must be flexible. If the going gets tough—and it will—General Petraeus must be given the latitude to employ U.S. forces in whatever fashion is required to avoid defeat for the elected government of Iraq. General Petraeus and American military forces can still achieve success in Iraq if the President, the American public and Congress support them. Do we have the patience and the guts? Significantly, two analysts who have harshly criticized the Bush administration's handling of Iraq filed a contributing editorial with *The New York Times* in late July 2007 stating that troop morale is high under General Petraeus and that "Here is the most important thing that Americans need to understand: We are finally getting somewhere in Iraq, at least in military terms."[21] Some would say we can win by not losing. We will not lose if we stay long enough in Iraq for the elected government to reduce the violence to a manageable level. We will not lose in Iraq unless Congress cuts off funds for the war (as they did in the Vietnam War). For the present and future security of Iraq, the region, and the United States, we cannot afford to lose in Iraq. If we lose in Iraq, we can expect the terrorists to follow us home.

To be realistic, there is also a real chance that the new strategy and tactics in Iraq will not work. The obstacles and challenges are monumental. Despite superhuman efforts by General Petraeus and our American soldiers, they may not receive the support from the U.S. Congress that they so justifiably deserve and need. The Iraqi people may not recognize, in time, that America has given it a great gift—it has rescued them from tyranny and offered them a future of hope, human dignity, and economic opportunity. The radical Muslim leaders and sects may not recognize, in time, that they are not really true to Islam, and that they are destroying themselves and the future of their children. The leaders of Saudi Arabia, Egypt, Jordan and the Gulf states may not recognize, until it is too late, that they should

---

[21] Michael E. O'Hanlon and Kenneth M. Pollack, "A War We Just Might Win," *New York Times*, July 30, 2007.

have acted far more decisively to support America and the U.K. in the War in Iraq and the War on Terror. They may be destroyed as leaders in the Middle East. The leaders of the European Union and NATO may not realize, until it is too late, that they should have given their full support to the U.S. and the U.K. in the Iraq War and the War on Terror. They may be destroyed as leaders and their people may lose their way of life. The leaders and the people of the rest of the world may not realize, until it is too late, that international terrorists, **who are nothing more than international criminals deceptively hiding in the cloak of Islam,** have the potential to destroy the way of life of the entire world. Finally, even Americans, who treasure freedom and democracy, may not recognize in time, that Congress and the entire country must support the President (whoever that might be) and U.S. military forces as they fight the War in Iraq and Afghanistan, and the War on Terror. If and when the U.S. withdraws its troops from Iraq and Afghanistan, U.S. leaders must still be prepared to confront and defeat militant Islamist terrorists who attack the U.S. at home or who attack U.S. interests abroad. There is no other rational choice. American voters must demand to know the positions (and plans) of Democratic and Republican presidential candidates regarding national defense in advance of elections. We cannot afford to elect a weak president.

I have the utmost admiration for the courage and competence of American military forces as they fight the terrorists and insurgents in Iraq, Afghanistan and around the world. What I treasure most in my memories of the Nimrods is that they had guts. Remember the Battle of the Bulge and the reply of General Anthony "Tony" McAuliffe at Bastogne when the advancing Nazi army surrounded his soldiers and arrogantly gave him an ultimatum to surrender. His reply was "Nuts!" You have to have guts to say "Nuts" to a Nazi army that has you surrounded. In World War II, we lost more than 405,000 men in combat (we lost 19,276 American soldiers in the Battle of the Bulge alone). I personally lost my father in the Battle of the Bulge, an indescribable loss, but he did not die in vain. Neither did thousands of other Americans die in vain in World War II. Hitler was defeated and America and the world remained free. Freedom is not free.

No doubt you have noticed, our American soldiers, marines, sailors and airmen still have guts, and they have the best equipment and

159

training in the world. If America loses its nerve and withdraws from Iraq and the Middle East, we will have to rely even more on our military forces to defend the United States at home. That means that our active duty military forces, and reserve and guard forces, will be called upon to "go all-out" to defeat terrorists on American soil. Such a war will extend well beyond military forces. We will also need to rely heavily on state and local law enforcement agencies (i.e., state, county and city police departments and their SWAT teams), and we will need to rely on "ordinary" American citizens all across America. It will be a total war at the local, state and national levels. The primary threats to Americans at home will be nuclear threats (either from an enemy nation's nuclear military forces, or from an enemy nation's terrorist proxies). We must prepare to meet and defeat those nuclear threats at all levels. However, major secondary threats will involve terrorists using chemical, biological and conventional bombs and bullets throughout our country.

Khalid Sheikh Mohammed, the self-confessed "mastermind" of the September 11, 2001, attacks on the United States (along with Osama bin Laden), claimed after his capture that al Qaeda was planning many more attacks against the United States. If we reach the point that America suffers repeated terrorist attacks, the entire country will be forced to mobilize and fight, as we did in World War II, to defeat determined tyrants obsessed with terrorism and domination of the entire world. One major difference, of course, is that we will be fighting at home. If that American response is too little too late, and if the terrorists should obtain nuclear weapons, the world could be approaching the time of the great battle of Armageddon (see language below quoted from the Book of Revelation of the Bible).

***

"12 And the sixth angel poured out his vial upon the great river Euphrates; and the water thereof was dried up, that the way of the kings of the east might be prepared. 13 And I saw three unclean spirits like frogs come out of the mouth of the dragon, and out of the mouth of the beast, and out of the mouth of the false prophet. 14 For they are the spirits of devils, working miracles, which go forth unto the kings of the earth and of the whole world, to gather them to the battle of that great day of

God Almighty. 15 Behold, I come as a thief. Blessed is he that watcheth, and keepeth his garments, lest he walk naked, and they see his shame. 16 And he gathered them together into a place called in the Hebrew tongue Armageddon." [Rev.16:12-16]

***

"11 And I saw heaven opened, and behold a white horse; and he that sat upon him was called Faithful and True, and in righteousness he doth judge and make war. 12 His eyes were as a flame of fire, and on his head were many crowns; and he had a name written, that no man knew, but he himself. 13 And he was clothed with a vesture dipped in blood: and his name is called the Word of God. 14 And the armies which were in heaven followed him upon white horses, clothed in fine linen, white and clean. 15 And out of his mouth goeth a sharp sword, that with it he should smite the nations: and he shall rule them with a rod of iron: and he treadeth the winepress of the fierceness and wrath of Almighty God. 16 And he hath on his vesture and on his thigh a name written, KING OF KINGS, AND LORD OF LORDS. 17 And I saw an angel standing in the sun; and he cried with a loud voice, saying to all the fowls that fly in the midst of heaven, Come and gather yourselves together unto the supper of the great God; 18 That ye may eat the flesh of kings, and the flesh of captains, and the flesh of mighty men, and the flesh of horses, and of them that sit on them, and the flesh of all men, both free and bond, both small and great. 19 And I saw the beast, and the kings of the earth, and their armies, gathered together to make war against him that sat on the horse, and against his army. 20 And the beast was taken, and with him the false prophet that wrought miracles before him, with which he deceived them that had received the mark of the beast, and them that worshipped his image. These both were cast alive into a lake of fire burning with brimstone. 21 And the remnant were slain with the sword of him that sat upon the horse, which sword proceeded out of his mouth: and all the fowls were filled with their flesh." [Rev.19:11-21]

The Old Testament of the Bible, particularly the Books of Daniel (see chapters 10-12) and Ezekiel (see chapters 38-39) contain extensive prophecies concerning the end times and the Battle of Armageddon. I will not quote them here but highly recommend that you read those passages as well as the Book of Revelation. As the civilized world continues to be stunned by the savage brutality and evil of radical Islamic tyrants and terrorists in the Middle East and in countries around the world, and as the Middle East continues to experience unrelenting warfare, religious leaders and scholars are warning people that the end times may be unfolding before our eyes. Americans must recognize the extreme dangers posed by these threats and unite to defend our citizens and our friends, at home and abroad. Christians must also recognize the urgency of our times and become stronger in their faith. Freedom of religion in America, and the willingness of Americans to respect all world religions that practice their faiths in a non-violent manner, are fundamental American values. Our American values and vision are worth fighting for. We must unite at home and join allies abroad to defeat terrorism and tyrants.

I came across the quoted language below (writer not identified) while doing some computer research. This language did not originate with me, but merits serious consideration by everyone concerned about the dangers to world security threatened by tyrants and terrorists operating in the Middle East and other parts of the world.

"The time draws near ... the Bible warns Iran (Persia), with Russia ('Magog' ... *who the Bible warns will also act as a 'guard'*), and a coalition of allies (including Turkey) *will* attack and will invade Israel. In Ezekiel 38-39 the Bible warns this coming war between Iran (Persia) and Israel will take place sometime *after* Israel has been re-gathered into Her land as a nation (which was fulfilled on May 14, 1948) ... this prophetic war has never yet taken place ... the only time in history Persia (Iran) has ever gone to war against Israel was to *help* Israel throw off the yoke of the Byzantine Empire around 614 AD. According to the Bible, Israel must stand alone...with God. Many Bible scholars believe that when this coming war *does* finally start,

162

the United States (for reasons yet unknown) will be unable or unwilling to help Israel defend herself. Although the Bible warns the invading armies will be ultimately destroyed by God, it will be a *devastating* war for both Israel and the whole world. Bible scholars are divided as to whether this coming war is part of the prophetic battle of Armageddon or will just precede the battle of Armageddon in order to prepare the path for the coming Antichrist (a coming 'world leader' who will enforce a 'peace plan' upon Israel). Bible students should be sitting on the edge of their seats with white knuckles watching this terrible prophecy slowly start to unfold ... while believing Christians (followers ... both Jew and Gentile ... of Jesus-Yeshua, the promised Messiah) are told to 'examine' themselves in the Word and in faith to insure they are not just 'almost' Christians (followers of the Messiah) or 'luke warm' in their faith ... for Jesus-Yeshua the Messiah warns all to, "Watch, therefore, and pray always (not just sometimes), that you will be counted worthy to *escape* all these things (the terrible events of the coming 'Apocalypse') that *will* come to pass" ... (Luke 21:36) ... for the Bible promises believing Christians (faithful believers and followers of the Messiah) who are alive at that time and have endured in their faith in God's Word are *not* 'appointed' to this coming time of 'God's wrath' that will be 'poured out' upon the whole world ... (1 Thessalonians 1:10 ... 1 Thessalonians 5:9-11)"[22]

Roger D. Graham

---

[22] Israel Nat'l News: www.alphanewsdaily.com/index.html

APPENDICES

APPENDIX A:
A/B-26 MEMORIAL

The memorial plaque shown on the next page shows the names of A/B-26 crewmembers who lost their lives while flying the A-26 or B-26 from 1961 to 1969. The actual memorial is open to visitors at Hurlburt Field, an Air Force Special Operations installation located near Ft. Walton Beach, Florida. I did not know all of the individuals whose names are listed on the memorial, but I did have the privilege of flying with many of them at England AFB, Louisiana and Nakhon Phanom Royal Thai Air Force Base, Thailand in the 1967-68 time period. During the course of writing this book, I learned that Captain Dwight S. Campbell and Captain Robert L. Sholl lost their lives while flying as Nimrod 36 in the pre-dawn darkness of February 22, 1967. On that date, their heroism is credited with saving the lives of two other Nimrod crewmembers when explosions resulted in the crash of Nimrod 36 just east of the airfield at NKP. Additionally, Major James E. Sizemore and Major Howard F. Andre lost their lives after departing NKP for a night mission in Laos on July 8, 1969. As their A-26 Invader made a strafing pass on a communist target in rugged jungle-covered mountains, the aircraft was struck by ground fire and exploded immediately upon impact with the ground.

The names of all American service members who lost their lives in the Vietnam War may be located at the Vietnam Memorial website, www. war-stories.com/wall-h.htm. Another website, www.tlc-brotherhood. org, contains vast amounts of Vietnam War information and links pertaining to Thailand, Laos and Cambodia. For an outstanding A-26 Nimrod legacy website, see www.a-26legacy.org. If you are a computer flight simulation enthusiast, you may fly the A-26 and B-52 by making an internet connection to www.flightsim.com and downloading the two aircraft (and many others) to Microsoft Flight Simulator 2004. Both the A-26 and B-52 work exceptionally well with Flight Simulator 2004. I hope they will be modified for use with Microsoft Flight Simulator X as soon as possible.

IN HONOR OF OUR COMRADES

LOST IN THE A/B-26

1961-1969

Howard F. Andre	Cleveland Gordon	Robert E. Pietsch
John P. Bartley	Louis F. Guillermin	William J. Potter
Arthur E. Bedal	George B. Hertlein	Howard P. Purcell
Robert D. Bennett	Vincent J. Hickman	Robert L. Scholl
Garry W. Bitton	Bruce A. Jensen	John F. Shaughnessy Jr.
John W. Callahan	John C. Kerr	James E. Sizemore
Jerry A. Campaigne	Atis K. Lielmanis	Francis E. Smiley
Dwight S. Campbell	Lawrence L. Lively	Jerry D. Stout
Anthony F. Cavalli	John H. McClean	Ronald E. Suladie
Howard R. Cody	James McMahon	Miles T. Tanimoto
Carlos R. Cruz	Andrew C. Mitchell	William B. Tully
Raphael Cruz	Carl B. Mitchell	David H. Tyndale
Robert C. Davis	Neal E. Monette	Eugene J. Waldvogel
Charles S. Dudley	Herman S. Moore	Thomas R. White
George "Glen" Duke	Burke H. Morgan	James W. Widdis
Paul Foster	James R. O'Neill	Thomas W. Wolfe

APPENDIX B:
NIMROD HISTORY
DOCUMENT

Before writing this book, I submitted a Freedom of Information Act (FOIA) request to the Air Force Historical Research Agency for documents pertaining to A-26 operations in the Vietnam War. The only document sent to me in response to my FOIA request was a document that I wrote as the 609th Special Operations Squadron Historical Officer covering the period July 1 – September 30, 1968. The Commander's Conclusion was written by Lt. Colonel John J. Shippey, Squadron Commander. That document was declassified before it was released in response to my FOIA request. I am including a copy of that document with this book because of its historical value, and because it was written contemporaneously with our combat tour of duty in 1967-68.

DEPARTMENT OF THE AIR FORCE
AIR FORCE HISTORICAL RESEARCH AGENCY
MAXWELL AIR FORCE BASE, ALABAMA

01 November, 2004

HQ AFHRA/RSA   Re: 32181/FOIA 05-002
600 Chennault Circle
Maxwell AFB AL 36112-6424

Mr. Roger D. Graham
█████████████████

Dear Mr. Graham:

This is in response to your Freedom Of Information request dated 06 October, 2004, and given FOIA # 05-002. A check of the 609th Air Commando Squadron histories produced one history for the period 1 July-30 September 1968 that was written by Roger D. Graham, Capt, USAF. I have attached a copy of that history for your perusal. There are no such histories as "A-26 histories." The attached history may or may not mention "A-26."

I hope this information is helpful.

Sincerely,

Mickey Russell
Mickey Russell
Archives Branch
William.russell@maxwell.af.mil
(334) 953-5068

Attachments:
1. Jul-Sep 1968 609th Air Commando Sq history.

172

RETURN TO:

HISTORY

OF

56th SPECIAL OPERATIONS WING

1 July - 30 September 1968

(Unclassified Title)

Assigned to:

Seventh/Thirteenth Air Force, Thirteenth Air Force, Pacific Air Force

Stationed at:

Nakhon Phanom Royal Thai Air Force Base, Thailand

P.R.C.

Richard S. Stotts   Edwin J. White Jr.
RICHARD S. STOTTS 30 Sep 88   EDWIN J. WHITE JR.
MSgt, USAF   Colonel, USAF
Historian   Commander

Copy No. 1 of 5 copies

2-9960-1

451123

HISTORICAL DATA RECORD
(RCS: AU-D5)

REPORTING PERIOD
From: 1 Jul 1968
TO: 30 Sep 1968

FROM: 609th Special Operations Squadron (OPS)
APO San Francisco 96310

TO: 56 SpOpWg (OPS)

G

I. MISSION:

a. Primary: To conduct combat operations as directed.

b. Secondary: To fly armed reconnaissance, flare support and FAC missions to disrupt and harass enemy lines of communications by attacking or directing attacks on pre-selected targets and targets of opportunity in the Steel Tiger (including Tiger Hound) and Barrel Roll areas of Laos.

II. PERSONNEL STATUS: (As of 30 Sep 1968)

	Officers	Airmen	Civilians	Total
Assigned	40	115	0	155
Authorized	41	100	0	141
Attached	0	0	0	0
MIA	0 (This reporting period)			
KIA	0 (This reporting period)			

III. Equipment Status:

Nomenclature	No. Asgd	Gains	Losses	Reasons
Truck, Multi-Stop 4x2	1	-	-	-
Truck, Pickup, 3 pass.	1	-	-	-
A-26 Aircraft	14	2	-	(1 of 14 assigned undergoing repairs- landing accident)

IV. SIGNIFICANT STATISTICS:

a. Total Combat Flying Hours — 1958 + 50

b. Total Combat Sorties Scheduled — 865

c. Total Combat Sorties Flown — 756

CY# 1 of 6 cys
609-68-S-008

d. Sorties Cancelled Due to Adverse Weather   55

e. Sorties Cancelled Due to Maintenance   15

f. Sorties Cancelled Due to BBQ   39

MUNITIONS EXPENDED:

Description	Amount
MK81 (250 lb GP Bomb)	409
MK82 (500 lb GP Bomb)	54
M117 (750 lb GP Bomb)	52
M1A4 (Fragmentation Bomb Cluster)	5,290
BLU-10 (250 lb Unfinned Fire Bomb)	130
BLU-27 (750 lb Finned Fire Bomb)	214
BLU-23 (500 lb Finned Fire Bomb)	70
BLU-32 (500 lb Finned Fire Bomb)	2,344
M-31, M-32 (500 lb Incendiary Bomb Cluster)	236
CBU 14/A (Cluster Bomb Unit)	1,295
CBU 25 (Cluster Bomb Unit, Foliage Penetrating)	128
CBU 29 (750 lb Cluster Bomb Unit, Delay Fused)	8
CBU 24 (750 lb Cluster Bomb Unit, Impact Fused)	60
LAU-3 (Rocket Pod)	42
50 Cal. (API Ammunition)	167,050

TARGETS STRUCK:

Description	Amount
Trucks	925
AAA Guns	105
Road Segments	10
Troop Concentrations	63
Troop/Storage Area	132
Truck Parks	183
Boats/Barges	7/9
Bulldozer	1

STRIKE RESULTS:

Description	Amount
Trucks Destroyed	287
Trucks Probably Destroyed	29
Trucks Damaged	6
AAA Guns Silenced	53
AAA Guns Destroyed	4
Secondary Fires	1,632
Secondary Explosions	580
Road Interdictions	6
Boats/Barges Destroyed	9/1

AIRCRAFT STATUS:

	July	August	September
OR	75.7%	55.5%	62.8%
NORM	24.3%	44.5%	37.2%
NORS	LESS 5%	LESS 5%	LESS 5%

V. NARRATIVE:

During this quarter, Nimrod crews of the 609th Special Operations
Squadron, flying A-26 Attack Bomber aircraft, continued their night
armed reconnaissance operations in the Steel Tiger/Tiger Hound areas
of East-Central Laos and in the Barrel Roll area of Northeast Laos.
Crews of the 609th were restricted from flying missions into the
southern panhandle of North Vietnam, and were prohibited from violating a ten mile buffer zone along the North Vietnam border north of
19 degrees latitude in the Barrel Roll area. The high level of supply
truck movement along the Ho Chi Minh Trail of last quarter was significantly reduced during this quarter, the primary cause being the heavy
rains associated with the Southwest Monsoon. Weather personnel recorded
a total of 42.92 inches of rain during this three month period, which
damaged certain route segments to the extent that truck traffic was
either impossible or greatly hindered.

As in the past, Nimrod crews operating in the Steel Tiger/Tiger
Hound areas concentrated on destroying moving supply trucks bound for
enemy North Vietnam and Vietcong military forces in South Vietnam; and
in the case of crews operating in Barrel Roll the primary effort was
still to destroy moving supply trucks heading for enemy North Vietnam
and Pathet Lao forces which are mainly concentrated in the Plaines Des
Jarres region of Northern Laos, but which are also encountered in

various locations depending on rapidly changing enemy military objectives
in that region. Nimrod crews abandoned their primary effort of destroying
moving enemy supply trucks only to come to the aid of friendly Royal
Laotian ground forces that were either under direct attack by North
Vietnam and/or Pathet Lao units, or if it was determined that attack
on friendly positions was imminent. Secondary targets included AAA
positions, road interdictions, and intelligence pre-briefed truck park/
storage areas. As a last resort ordnance was dropped under the direction
of ground radar sites (Combat Skyspot) when weather prevented visual
target acquisition.

Although Nimrod crews have the authority to FAC themselves in on
target strikes their ability to do so is limited because of the lack
of A-26 electronic aids; they have neither light amplification devices
(Starlight Scopes) nor radar, but must rely on visual target acquisition
from flarelight, or in some cases by moonlight. As a result of these
limitations, A-26 crews are almost completely dependant upon specialized
FAC crews, such as the C-123 Candlesticks, the O2A/B Nails, and the C-130
Lamplighters and Blindbats, who do have the capability to acquire and
mark targets by using light amplification devices and radar (O-2A does
not have radar). Nimrod crews have no doubt that their success is
heavily dependent on close coordination with FAC aircrews who locate and
mark targets. In some cases, primarily in Barrel Roll, target strikes
result from coordination with friendly ground teams who patrol the roads
and call in strike aircraft if they are able to spot moving trucks.

177

During this quarter a total of 756 combat sorties were flown by 609th crews. Of that number 537 were flown in the Steel Tiger/Tiger Hound areas and 219 were flown in Barrel Roll. The average sortie flying time was 2.6 hours, and the average time-over-target was 1.4 hours. Truck sightings, and consequently truck kills, were significantly reduced from the previous quarter. During the previous quarter (April - June), 831 trucks were destroyed by Nimrod crews. In comparison, only 925 trucks were struck during this quarter (July - September) and 287 of these trucks were destroyed. The 287 kills were either confirmed by FAC's with Starlight Scopes or by ground teams. As was previously stated, this reduction in activity was a direct result of the heavy monsoon rains. However, the level of truck movement and associated AAA defensive reactions greatly surpassed that of the July through September period of 1967. In fact, based on the experience of the July - September period of 1967, crews of the 609th expected truck movement and AAA reactions to come to a virtual standstill during July - September of this year. Such was not the case.

Route 912 from the North Vietnam border to where it intersects Route 911 at D-68 remained open to truck traffic almost constantly. Also, Route 911 from D-68 south to D-11 where it intersects Routes 9 and 914 remained open most of the time, as did Routes 9 and 914 from D-11 southeast to Khe Sanh in South Vietnam and south to the Cambodian border area. This route complex made up the main artery of enemy truck supply movement through the Steel Tiger/Tiger Hound areas of Laos south to South Vietnam.

Route 911/23 from the Mu Gia Pass south to D-68, which was heavily
travelled during the dry season, was almost completely abandoned as
a supply route during this quarter. The damage to supply routes in
Barrel Roll by heavy rains and flooding was negligible because of the
rugged, mountainous terrain of that region. In Barrel Roll Nimrod
crews concentrated on destroying trucks along Routes 6, 7, and 61
(See Attachment #3 for location of Steel Tiger/Tiger Hound, Barrel
Roll, and their associated routes).

The heaviest activity of this three month period occurred in July.
Although there were few truck strikes and associated AAA reactions during
the first week of July, the tempo of activity of the last three weeks
picked up considerably, which indicated that enemy forces were in urgent
need of more supplies in South Vietnam. This push to resupply occurred
despite the 12.21" of rain that fell on the dirt roads of the Ho Chi
Minh Trail during July. Some of the outstanding missions flown by
Nimrod crews are listed below. (1) Nimrod 35 on 14 July (Pilot -
Capt Michael J.C. Roth, FR70258 and Navigator Capt Roger D. Graham,
FR70029) destroyed six trucks while under fire from 4 x 37MM and 2 2FU
(14.5MM) guns. (2) Nimrods 35 and 37 on 19 July (Pilots were Major
Mark R. Richards, FR32062 and Capt Charles A. Kenyon, FR51001, and the
navigators were Capt Leroy D. Zarucchi, FV3129566, and Capt William A.
Cohen, FR55438) each destroyed 4 trucks. Nimrod 35 had 4 secondary
fires and 2 secondary explosions, and Nimrod 37 had 1 secondary fire
and seven secondary explosions. Their strikes occurred in the same
area and at about the same time. A total of 6 x 37MM guns fired at
them during the strikes.

179

(3) Nimrods 31 and 32 on 22 July (Pilots Lt Col John J. Shippey, FR39944, and Capt Bruce C. Wolfe, FR77247, and navigators Capt Leroy D. Zarucchi, FV3129566, and Capt Lawrence J. Elliott, FV3150643) each destroyed 6 trucks. Nimrod 31 was fired at by 3 AAA positions and Nimrod 32 noted 7 AAA positions active in his area. (4) Nimrod 32 on 24 July (Pilot - Major John A. Parrish, FR47852, and navigator - Capt William A. Cohen, FR55438) destroyed 5 trucks and had 2 secondary fires while being shot at by 1 x 37MM. (5) Nimrod 31 on 26 July (Pilot - Major John A Parrish, FR47852, and navigator Capt Frank W. Nelson, FR3139297) destroyed 4 trucks and had 3 secondary fires, and 5 secondary explosions while being fired at by 1 x 37MM. (6) Nimrod 32 on 31 July (Pilot - Lt Col Atlee R. Ellis, FR18377, and navigator Capt William A. Cohen, FR55438), destroyed 1 x 37MM and silenced 2 x 37MM positions out of a total of 5 x 37MM positions that were firing at them. They also noted 4 secondary fires and numerous secondary explosions.

A total of 84 trucks were confirmed destroyed during August, which was a significant reduction from the 136 truck kills during July. Little truck movement was observed during the first three weeks of August, mainly due to the 14.55" of rain that fell during the month. However, clearing weather the last week of August prompted another push by the enemy, especially along Route 912 of Steel Tiger. A tropical storm during the second week of August forced HHQ to cancel 25 missions. Only one truck was struck that week and none were destroyed. In general, crews were forced to increase the number of strikes on truck parks, either visually or under ground radar control (Combat Skyspot).

Some of the outstanding missions during August are as follows:

(1) Nimrod 38 on 27 August (Pilot - Major Lee D. Griffin, FV3034963, and navigator - Capt Ernest J. Wiedenhoff, FV3101926) destroyed 6 trucks and had 32 secondary fires and 6 secondary explosions.

(2) Nimrod 33 on 28 August (Pilot - Major Elmer E. Peters, FV3025999, and navigator - Capt Thomas E. Bronson, FR3160694) destroyed 4 of the 5 trucks they were attacking and had 1 secondary fire. A total of 4 x 37MM positions fired at them during their strikes.

(3) Nimrod 32 on 28 August (Pilot - Major John A. Parrish, FR47852, and navigator - Capt Lawrence J. Elliott, FV3150643) destroyed 4 trucks while under fire from 2 x 37MM positions.

Truck movement during September was lower than any other month of this reporting period, and lower than any month of the previous 12 months. Heavy typhoon rains fell on the enemy route structure during the first two weeks of September, but the weather gradually began clearing up the later part of the month indicating that the Southwest Monsoon was drawing to a close. A total of 16.16" of rain was recorded by weather personnel during September. However, Nimrod crews managed to destroy 67 trucks during the month despite poor weather conditions, and despite the fact that they were forced to work with reduced ordnance loads from the 5600 ft. parallel taxiway while the main 8000 ft. runway was being repaired. Three outstanding missions during the month are listed below:

(1) Nimrod 32 on 7 September (Pilot - Lt Col Robert L. Schultz, FR42560, and navigator - Capt Jerry L. Meek, FR82966) destroyed 2 trucks in Barrel Roll and probably destroyed 2 more.

(2) Nimrod 36 on 11 September (Pilot - Major Mark L. Richards, FR32062, and navigator - Capt Leroy D. Zarruchi, FV3129566) destroyed 9 boats and 1 barge loaded with POL; there were 15 secondary fires which burned for more than 45 minutes after the strike, and there was one secondary explosion. They were fired at by automatic weapons.

(3) Nimrod 31 on 19 September (Pilot - Major Albert Shortt, FR53228, and navigator - Capt Lawrence J. Counts, FR3129974) destroyed 4 trucks and observed one secondary explosion while being fired at by 1 x 37MM.

II. TACTICS:

Since the subject of tactics is too broad to cover in a report of this type, only the basic tactics used by Nimrod crews will be covered here. Night dive bombing combat missions in rugged terrain, and often in inclement weather, demand the highest level of pilot skill and pilot/navigator crew coordination. A crew must constantly be aware of their location, altitude, and the terrain elevation below. The 609th has continued the policy of making a maximum of 6 passes and releasing ordnance 5000 AGL when in high threat areas. Although AAA defenses were lighter during this quarter than during the previous three quarters, none of the 609th aircraft received battle damage during this quarter, which attests to the validity of this policy. Nimrod crews concentrated on killing trucks but made every reasonable effort to provide flak suppression for other strike aircraft. However, Nimrod crews have learned through experience that no matter how good their tactics and coordination with FAC crews are, their effectiveness is dictated by the type of ordnance load they have available.

182

Specifically, the most effective ordnance for night strikes, because of the large area coverage obtained, are incendiary bomb clusters of the M-31, M-32, and M-36 variety. Regrettably, this type of ordnance was in short supply this entire quarter and probably will be in the foreseeable future.

Two crewmembers, Major Daniel F. Grob (Pilot) and Major Robert W. Squires (Navigator), are assigned the additional duties of being Squadron Tactics Officers. They monitor tactics of the 609th, and about once a month squadron meetings are held to bring all crewmembers up to date on current tactics.

Lt Col Atlee R. Ellis, Squadron Operations Officer, attended a tactics conference at Bangkok on the 9th and 10th of September. Representatives of combat units from all over SEA who are directly involved in night combat operations were present at the conference. The purpose of the conference was to evaluate past night tactics and to come up with more effective tactics to be used in the coming dry season, which resulted in the drawing up of Operations Plan "Commando Hunt". Listed below are the basic points which Lt Col Ellis brought up at the conference:

(1) Incendiary ordnance preferred for night truck strikes (M-31 and M-32).

(2) Need more strike aircraft and more FACs.

(3) Need improved airspace control.

(4) Need more flak suppression.

(5) Expedite FAC supply of large Starlight Scopes.

(6) Request approval for hot pursuit of trucks across Route 912 at NVN border.

(7) Suggest B-57's use NKP for turnaround.

(8) Suggest firecan (radar) warnings be broadcast over guard frequency the same as MIG calls.

(9) Update photos of route structure every 30 days.

(10) Suggest timely BDA photographs be available to FAC aircrews.

(11) Eliminate coding of delta points to decrease confusion.

III. <u>MAINTENANCE</u>:

Interviews with the Squadron Maintenance Officer, 1st Lt James M. Collins, FV3180154, and the NCOIC of Maintenance, SMSgt James W. Pitsonberger, AF16381907, disclosed that 13 of the 14 A-26 aircraft are available to accomplish the mission. One aircraft (Tail #677) is out of commission as the result of a landing accident on 31 August. The pilot encountered a propellor reverse malfunction on a wet, slippery runway and was unable to keep the aircraft on the runway during the landing roll. The gear, nose, and propellers were damaged to the extent that this was considered a major accident. The pilot and navigator escaped injury, but approximately 5000 manhours will be required to make the aircraft operationally ready again. Only 15 sorties out of a scheduled 865 were cancelled because of maintenance, which is an outstanding record considering the fact that there were 50% turnover of maintenance personnel during this quarter. Maintenance was required to provide operationally ready aircraft for 9 sorties a night up until the last half of September when the requirement was raised to 10 sorties a night.

The major maintenance problem encountered during this quarter was the lack of specialists: there are 140 aircraft on base, but there are only enough specialists to take care of fewer than 100 aircraft. To help alleviate this problem, the 609th formed a five man engine team under the supervision of SSgt Lankford, which decreased the out of commission time because of engines by about 80%. Faulty electrical and comm-nav components, caused by rain leaking into the aircraft, was another major problem. Every attempt was made to keep the aircraft cockpit covered when the aircraft was not being flown. Certain parts, such as fuel flow transmitters, and BRIC units, were in short supply this quarter but this situation is improving.

IV. TRAINING:

A-26 aircrews received the bulk of their training at England AFB, La., but are required to complete a checkout program after they arrive at Nakhon Phanom RTAFB. The checkout program is controlled by the squadron commander and operations officer and is monitored by Capt. William A. Cohen, the 609th Training Officer. Pilots get an average of 7 checkout rides with instructors, and navigators get an average of 6 rides. There are 7 instructor pilots and 7 instructor navigators in the squadron who actually conduct this training. (See Attachment 2 for names of IP's and IN's)

The squadron combat ready status has remained at C-1 during this quarter except for two brief periods when PCS rotation temporarily dropped the rating to C-2 until additional crewmembers were checked out. At the end of this quarter, the rating was C-1 with 15 crews in combat ready status.

V. ARMAMENT:

1st Lt Robert Skipp, FV3180519, the 609th Armament Officer, provided the information that follows. The base has only about 250 M-31/M-32 bombs in stock and there are only about 700 bombs of this type scheduled to be delivered in the future. This is the best truck killing ordnance that Nimrod crews have used because of the large area coverage and intense heat of the weapon. A 750 lb version of this bomb, the M-36, is scheduled for production but will not be available in the near future.

Dud rates were low during this quarter except for BLU-23 napalm bombs (1 out of 4 were duds). The ingredients of this bomb were discovered to not be properly combined and this problem has been corrected. The flare (MK-24) dud rate has been greatly decreased by utilizing the SUU 25 B/A flare dispenser. Special emphasis has been placed on increasing the efficiency of the eight .50 caliber guns, i.e., they are cleaned and oiled daily and the fire-out rate has increased considerably.

A noteworthy change of procedure was initiated by armament personnel this quarter to increase safety. To prevent inadvertent firing of guns or release of ordnance the procedure of disconnecting batteries prior to loading and pulling the master arm circuit breaker was established.

VI. AWARDS AND DECORATIONS:

A total of 13 Silver Stars and 21 Distinguished Flying Crosses were presented to Nimrod crewmembers during this quarter (See attachment 2 for names of recipients). Other medals have been presented prior to this quarter, either at Nakhon Phanom RTAFB or at the crewmembers next PCS station.

The large majority of medals presented to date were awarded for missions
flown during the past dry season, i.e., November 1967 through May 1968.
The Silver Stars were presented by either General Nazzaro, General Momyer,
General Gideon, or General Brown, during various visits to Nakhon Phanom
RTAFB in this quarter. The DFC's were presented by Colonel McCoskris,
56th Sp Op Wg Commander, or by a member of his staff.

Major Kenneth E. LaFave, FR60712, was awarded the Thirteenth Air Force
"Well Done" plaque for his outstanding performance of duty as an A-26 pilot
on 11 May 1968. On that date Major LaFave's aircraft took a 37MM hit while
he was striking a truck convoy, but he managed to successfully fly the
seriously crippled aircraft back to Nakhon Phanom RTAFB for a safe landing.
(See Attachment #4).

VII. COMMANDERS CONCLUSION:

I, Lt Col John J. Shippey, FR39944, replaced Lt Col Robert E. Brumm,
FR17717, as the Squadron Commander of the 609th Air Commando Squadron on
18 July 1968. (See Attachment 5). On 1 August 1968, the 609th Air
Commando Squadron was redesignated as the 609th Special Operations Squadron.
(See Attachment 6). The squadron effectiveness has remained high due to
many factors. Continuing emphasis is placed on training of newly arrived
crewmembers, as well as improving tactics for all. The imposition by the
56th Sp Op Wg of a 5000 ft minimum release altitude for ordnance delivery
in high threat areas caused some difficulties for a short period, but
modified tactics were rapidly adopted by all crews and our bombing accuracy
was not significantly degraded. Adverse weather conditions prevailing
throughout the reporting period due to the Southwest Monsoon season
drastically reduced truck movement and opposing gunfire, however, this

has still been the most active monsoon season reported since the A-26's began working in our operating areas.

Improved FAC'ing has been continually provided, primarily by the "Candle Sticks", the C-123 FAC's of the 606th Sp Op Sq.

The limitations imposed in the Barrel Roll area, i.e., no strikes within the 10 mile buffer zone, being fragged only to limited areas of the Bravo and Cocoa areas (Routes 7, 6 and 61), and the fact that TACAN is available as a navigational aid only when approximately 50% of the time in the area caused some decrease in our effectiveness in the northern area.

Maintenance difficulties were a major source of concern throughout the period, caused primarily by a severe shortage of qualified technicians. Flight line personnel absorbed a great deal of work normally accomplished by specialists which prevented the loss of many missions. The flight line personnel, both maintenance and munitions loading, worked many hours of overtime under the worst possible conditions to continue our effort at a maximum rate. They are to be very highly commended for an outstanding job.

Our squadron OJT Program improved drastically, due primarily to the efforts of TSgt Duncan, the Squadron Training NCO. Through his training program and the efforts of supervisors within the organization, 11 individuals of 13 tested, passed.

JOHN J. SHIPPEY, Lt Colonel, USAF
Commander

ROGER D. GRAHAM, Capt, USAF
Unit Historical Officer

SUPPORTING DOCUMENTS:

1. Nakhon Phanom RTAFB Form 20 (Pilots Mission Debriefing Form, 609th Sp Op Sq Records). Confidential.

2. 609th Sp Op Sq Weekly Summary Reports. July, August, September of 1968.

3. 609th Sp Op Sq Flight Orders. (609th Sp Op Sq Records).

4. Attachment 1: Roster of Key Personnel.

5. Attachment 2: Roster of 609th Crewmembers.

6. Attachment 3: Familiarization Map of Laos.

7. Attachment 4: Thirteenth Air Force "Well Done" Award.

8. Attachment 5: Special Order #14.

9. Attachment 6: Special Order G-167

189

ATTACHMENT 1

ROSTER OF 609TH KEY PERSONNEL

Squadron Commander	Lt Col John J. Shippey
Operations Officer	Lt Col Atlee R. Ellis
Administrative & Executive Officer	Major Kenneth E. LaFave
"A" Flight Commander	Major Robert F. Bennett
"B" Flight Commander	Major Daniel F. Grob
"C" Flight Commander	Major Douglas W. Carmichael
"D" Flight Commander	Lt Col Robert L. Schultz
Maintenance Officer	1st Lt James M. Collins
NCOIC Maintenance	SMSgt James W. Pitsonberger
Armament Officer	1st Lt Robert Skipp
NCOIC Armament	MSgt Clarence H. Turk
Squadron 1st Sergeant	TSgt James M. Spivey

ATTACHMENT 2

PILOTS

Bennett, Robert F., Major, FR60166	(IP)	DFC
Bright, Jack W., Capt, FR62533		
Brumm, Robert E., Lt Col, FR17717		DFC
Carmichael, Douglas W., Major, FR44621	(IP)	DFC
Disteldorf, Bernard N., Major, FR58260	(IP)	
Ellis, Atlee R., Lt Col, FR18377		DFC
Fitzgerald, James C., Major, FR56827		
Grob, Daniel F., Major, FR45960	(IP)	SS, DFC
Griffin, Lee D., Major, FV3034963		
Kenyon, Charles A., Capt, FR51001	(IP)	
LaFave, Kenneth E., Major, FR60712		SS, DFC
Litton, Delbert W., Major, FR47196	(IP)	
Norton, Jay L., Capt, FR63672		SS
Parrish, John A., Major, FR47852		SS, DFC
Peters, Elmer E., Major, FV3025999		
Richards, Mark R., Major, FR32062		SS, DFC
Roth, Michael J.C., Capt, FR70258		(departed PCS August)
Schultz, Robert L., Lt Col, FR42560		
Sears, Bobby J., Major, FR47177	(SEFE/IP)	SS, DFC
Shippey, John J., Lt Col, FR39944		SS, DFC
Shortt, Albert, Major, FR53228		
Tengan, Seijun, Major, FR72019		SS (departed PCS August)
Vogler, Charles C., Major, FR53888		
Wolfe, Bruce R., Capt, FR77247		DFC (departed PCS August)
Yancey, Kenneth E., Major, FR65191		

NAVIGATORS

Bowman, Peter R., Major, FR72766		
Bronson, Thomas E., Capt, FR3160694	(IN)	DFC
Cohen, William A., Capt, FR55438	(IN)	DFC
Counts, Lawrence J., Capt, FR3129974		
Elliott, Lawrence J., Capt, FV3150643		DFC (departed PCS September)
Gierhart, Loran W., Major, FR30028	(IN)	
Graham, Roger D., Capt, FR70029		SS, DFC
Henry, Michael D., Capt, FV3118238		
Langford, Walter M. Jr, Major, FR47973	(SEFE/IN)	
Laws, Charles P., Capt, FR57922		
Meek, Jerry L., Capt, FR82966		
Nelson, Frank W., Capt, FR3139297	(IN)	SS, DFC
Richeal, James E., Major, FV3024881		
Squires, Robert W., Major, FR57833		SS, DFC
Watson, Marion R., Major, FR47641		
Willems, Richard L., Capt, FR3151684	(IN)	
Wiedenhoeff, Ernest J., Capt, FV3101926		
Zarucchi, Leroy D., Capt, FV3129566	(IN)	SS, DFC
Zimmerman, Robert G., Major, FR61238		SS, DFC (departed PCS Sept)
Wolf, Norman D., Capt, FV3151066		

CHINA

NORTH VIETNAM

LAOS

ROUTE 6 & 61

BARREL ROLL

PLAINES DES JARRES

ROUTE 7

MU GIA PASS

ROUTE 912

STEEL TIGER

NAKHON PHANOM RTAFB

+DMZ

ROUTE 911

ROUTE 9

ROUTE 914

TIGER HOUND

THAILAND

CAMBODIA

SOUTH VIETNAM

192

1 AUG 1968

REPLY TO
ATTN OF: DSA

SUBJECT: Thirteenth Air Force "Well Done" Award

TO: 56 Air Commando Wg (C)

1. Major Kenneth E. LaFave, FR60712, 56 Air Commando Wing, is awarded
the Thirteenth Air Force "Well Done" plaque for outstanding performance
of duty as pilot of an A-26 aircraft on 11 May 1968.

2. Major LaFave and Captain Cohen, pilot and navigator respectively of
an A-26 Attack Bomber, were performing an armed reconnaissance mission
in an AAA high threat area. Upon locating a truck convoy, the crew
commenced an attack. On their third pass, a 37MM shell hit the right
propeller and fuselage. The ensuing flak burst severely crippled the
aircraft and the shock wave shattered several of the navigator/co-pilot
instruments throwing glass throughout the cockpit. Major LaFave
immediately jettisoned his remaining ordnance on a gun position and
fought to control the aircraft which was vibrating and buffeting
severely. With great difficulty Major LaFave managed to return the
aircraft to straight and level flight. At this point, however the
number two engine fuel warning light came on and fuel pressure on
number two engine began to fluctuate rapidly. Captain Cohen switched
fuel tanks in an effort to preclude failure of the engine and after a
few seconds the fuel warning light did go out and fuel pressure settled
down to normal. Then number one engine commenced to lose power.
Captain Cohen switched fuel tanks on the number one engine which
caught and resumed normal operation as number two fuel warning light
again came on. Frequently during the forty-five minute flight to their
home base, Major LaFave almost lost out in his struggle to control the
severely damaged aircraft. However, he managed to find an optimum
power setting which permitted the best control with minimum aircraft
buffeting. As they approached the base and prepared for descent the
crew made a final inspection of the number two engine and elected to
keep it in operation for the landing due to the possible failure of
the number one engine. Major LaFave kept the approach high and made
a smooth touchdown. As soon as the wheels touched, Captain Cohen
quickly opened the cowl flaps and the clam shell doors of the canopy
for increased drag. As the aircraft came to a stop, number two
throttle control was lost and a lower stack on number two engine began
to flare and burn. Captain Cohen attempted to cut the number two
engine with the mixture lever but it continued to run at high RPM.
The engine had to finally be shut down by utilizing the fuel selector
lever.

193

3. Major LaFave's intimate knowledge of his aircraft and its capabilities, his immediate application of emergency procedures, and his outstanding professional airmanship resulted in the recovery of a valuable tactical aircraft. His commendable performance reflects great credit upon himself, this command, and the United States Air Force.

K. C. DEMPSTER, Major General, USAF
Vice Commander

1 Atch
13AF "Well Done" Award
(sep cover)

Cy to: Dep Cmdr 7/13AF

2

ATTACHMENT 5

DEPARTMENT OF THE AIR FORCE
609th Air Commando Squadron (PACAF)
APO San Francisco 96310

SPECIAL ORDER   18 July 1968
NO.   14

I, the undersigned, under the provisions of AFM 26-2, assume command of the
609th Air Commando Squadron effective this date.

JOHN J. SHIPPEY, Lt. Colonel, USAF   DISTRIBUTION
Commander   1 - All Sections 609th ACS
                                             1 - File

195

DEPARTMENT OF THE AIR FORCE
HEADQUARTERS PACIFIC AIR FORCES
APO SAN FRANCISCO 96553

SPECIAL ORDER
G-167.

11 July 1968

1. Effective 1 August 1968, the following units are redesignated as indicated with no change in location.

HQ, 14 Air Commando Wg	HQ, 14 Special Operations Wg
HQ, 56 Air Commando Wg	HQ, 56 Special Operations Wg
HQ, 315 Air Commando Wg	HQ, 315 Special Operations Wg
3 Air Command Sq, Fire Support	3 Special Operations Sq
4 Air Command Sq, Fire Support	4 Special Operations Sq
5 Air Command Sq, Psychological Operations	5 Special Operations Sq
9 Air Command Sq, Psychological Operations	9 Special Operations Sq
12 Air Command Sq, Defoliation	12 Special Operations Sq
15 Air Command Sq, Defoliation	15 Special Operations Sq
609 Air Command Sq, Defoliation	609 Special Operations Sq
606 Air Commando Sq, Composite	606 Special Operations Sq
1 Air Commando Sq, Fighter	1 Special Operations Sq
604 Air Commando Sq, Fighter	604 Special Operations Sq
19 Air Commando Sq, Tactical Airlift	19 Special Operations Sq
309 Air Commando Sq, Tactical Airlift	309 Special Operations Sq
310 Air Commando Sq, Tactical Airlift	310 Special Operations Sq
311 Air Commando Sq, Tactical Airlift	311 Special Operations Sq
602 Fighter Sq, Commando	602 Special Operations Sq

a. Air Force Organization Status Change Report (RCS: HAF-01) will be submitted IAW AFR 20-49.

b. Authority: DAF (AFOMO 929n) Ltr, Redesignation of certain units assigned CINCPACAF, 5 July 1968.

2. Effective 15 July 1968, the 6 Air Commando Sq, Fighter is redesignated to 6 Special Operations Sq with no change in location. Authority: AFM 26-2.

FOR THE COMMANDER IN CHIEF

JOHN D. _____ JR., Colonel, USAF
Director _____ Administration

G-167

SPECIAL ORDER   8 January 1968
M-11

The following named officers, 609 ACS, this station, are authorized to
perform aircrew duties in type aircraft shown. Authority: AFM 60-1,
PACAFM 60-2 and PACAFR 60-6. The verbal order of the Commander on
1 Jan 68, is confirmed, exigencies of the service having been such as
to preclude the issuance of competent written orders in advance.

LTCOL ROBERT E. BRUMM, FR17717	A-26 Pilot
LTCOL ALLEN F. LEARMONTH, FR17682	A-26 Pilot
LTCOL HOWARD L. FARMER, FR42005	A-26 Pilot
LTCOL FRANCIS L. MCMULLEN, FV2215574	A-26 Navigator
LTCOL ATLEE R. ELLIS, FR18377	A-26 Pilot
LTCOL JOHN J. SHIPPEY, FR39944	A-26 Pilot
MAJOR JOHN A. PARRISH, FR47582	A-26 Pilot
MAJOR PETER J. CASELLA, FR1858069	A-26 Navigator
MAJOR ROBERT N. BAKKEN, FR25945	A-26 Pilot
MAJOR RICHARD A. SCHRAMM, FV2225538	A-26 Pilot
MAJOR DOUGLAS W. HAWKINS, FR65649	A-26 Navigator
MAJOR WILLIAM R. DAVIS, FR25049	A-26 Pilot
MAJOR BRYANT A. MURRAY, FR42531	A-26 Navigator
MAJOR EDWARD M. ROBINSON, FV1858858	A-26 Pilot
MAJOR THOMAS L. WICKSTROM, FV1860833	A-26 Navigator
MAJOR RICHARD J. MENDONCA, FV3035471	A-26 Pilot
MAJOR ROBERT C. ZIMMERMAN, FR61238	A-26 Navigator
MAJOR BENNIE L. HEATHMAN, FR47376	A-26 Pilot
MAJOR BOBBY J. SEARS, FR47177	A-26 Pilot
MAJOR ROBERT W. SQUIRES, FR57833	A-26 Navigator
CAPT DONALD J. MAXWELL, FR3072009	A-26 Navigator
CAPT JAMES J. WHIPPS, III, FR3109744	A-26 Navigator
CAPT THOMAS E. OWNES, FV3133367	A-26 Navigator
CAPT MICHAEL J. ROTH, FR70258	A-26 Pilot
CAPT BRUCE R. WOLFE, FR77247	A-26 Pilot
CAPT LOUIS F. GUILLERMIN, FV3150435	A-26 Navigator
CAPT ROBERT E. PIETSCH, FR67605	A-26 Pilot
CAPT SELJUN TENGAN, FR72019	A-26 Pilot
CAPT FRANK W. NELSON, FV3139297	A-26 Navigator
CAPT LEROY D. ZARUCCHI, FV3129566	A-26 Navigator
CAPT BERNARD N. DISTELDORF, FR58260	A-26 Pilot
CAPT ROGER D. GRAHAM, FR70029	A-26 Navigator
CAPT GEORGE B. HERTLEIN, III, FV3102462	A-26 Navigator
CAPT JAY L. NORTON, FR63672	A-26 Pilot
1STLT LAURENCE J. ELLIOTT, FV3150643	A-26 Navigator
1STLT RICHARD L. WILLEMS, FV3151684	A-26 Navigator

FOR THE COMMANDER   DISTRIBUTION
                                      5 - Indiv
                                      5 - CBPO
     OFFICIAL   10 - 609 ACS
                                      1 - 13AF
DONALD C. ROUNTREE, Capt, USAF   1 - File
Chief, Administrative Services

197

NIMROD PILOTS

PIE	CAPT ROBERT E. PIETSCH	MAY 68	MIA 30 APR 68
MEN	MAJOR RICHARD MENDONCA	MAY 68	
FAR	LTCOL HOWARD L. FARMER	MAY 68	C.O. 1 AUG 67-1 JAN 68
BAK	MAJOR ROBERT W. BAKKEN	JUN 68	
HEA	MAJOR BENNIE L. HEATHMAN	JUN 68	
SCH	MAJOR RICHARD P. SCHRAMM	JUL 68	
ROT	CAPT MICHAEL J. ROTH	JUL 68	
ROB	MAJOR EDWARD M. ROBINSON	JUL 68	
WOL	CAPT BRUCE R. WOLFE	AUG 68	
TEN	CAPT SEIJUN TENGAN	SEP 68	
LAF	MAJOR KENNETH E. LAFAVE	OCT 68	
PAR	MAJOR JOHN A. PARRISH	OCT 68	
SHI	LTCOL JOHN J. SHIPPEY	NOV 68	C.O. 1 JUL-1 NOV 68
BRU	LTCOL ROBERT L. BRUMM	NOV 68	C.O. 1 JAN-1 JUL 68
ELL	LTCOL ATLEE R. ELLIS	NOV 68	C.O. 1 NOV-5 NOV 68
SEA	MAJOR BOBBY J. SEARS	NOV 68	
DIS	MAJOR BERNARD N. DISTELDORF	NOV 68	
RIC	MAJOR MARK R. RICHARDS	NOV 68	
BEN	MAROR ROBERT F. BENNETT	DEC 68	
NOR	CAPT JAY L. NORTON	DEC 68	
GRO	MAJOR DANIEL F. GROB	DEC 68	
CAR	LTCOL DOUGLAS W. CARMICHAEL	APR 69	O.O. 1 NOV 68-1 APR 69
LIT	MAJOR DELBERT W. LITTON	MAY 69	
KEN	MAJOR CHARLES A. KENYON	JUN 69	
GRI	MAJOR LEE D. GRIFFIN	JUN 69	
SCH	LTCOL ROBERT L. SCHULTZ	JUL 69	C.O. 5 NOV 68-1 JUL 69
PET	MAJOR ELMER E. PETERS	JUL 69	
SHO	MAJOR ALBERT SHORTT	JUL 69	O.O. 1 APR-1 JUL 69
FIT	MAJOR JAMES G. FITZGERALD	JUL 69	
VOG	MAJOR CHARLES C. VOGLER	SEP 69	
YAN	MAJOR KENNETH E. YANCEY	SEP 69	
ROB	CAPT ROSCOE R. ROBERTS III	MAY 69	
WAR	MAJOR MILTON J. WARNER	OCT 69	
DIX	MAJOR ROBERT L. DIXON	NOV 69	
BAT	MAJOR CHARLES T. BATES	NOV 69	
HOT	CAPT ANTHONY M. HOTSKO	NOV 69	
JEF	MAJOR JOE A. JEFFERIS	DEC 69	
MAR	CAPT PAUL M. MARSCHALK	DEC 69	
WID	CAPT JAMES W. WIDDIS	DEC 69	MIA 21 MAR 69
MON	CAPT NEAL E. MONETTE	DEC 69	KIA 12 MAR 69
PEE	LTCOL FLOYD A. PEEDE	MAR 69	
SIZ	MAJOR JAMES E. SIZEMORE	JAN 70	KIA 4 JUL 69
STO	LTCOL ROBERT W. STOUT	MAR 70	C.O. 1 JUL 69
LOR	MAJOR WILLIAM H. LORIMAR	MAR 70	
KOY	MAJOR DANIEL W. KOYN	MAR 70	
PAR	CAPT EDDIE L. PARRIS	MAR 70	
SON	CAPT PETER F. PETERSON	MAR 70	

MAU	MAJOR HENRY J. MAULDIN	MAR 70
KIN	CAPT MICHAEL KING	APR 70
MAS	MAJOR ROBERT C. MASON	MAY 70
KEL	MAJOR RICHARD G. KELLER	MAY 70
RIL	MAJOR FRANCIS E. RILEY	JUN 70

NIMROD NAVIGATOR/CO-PILOTS

OWE	CAPT THOMAS E. OWENS	JUN 68	
HER	CAPT GEORGE B. HERTLEIN III	JUN 68	KIA 24 APR 68
GUI	CAPT LOUIS F. GUILLERMIN	JUN 68	MIA 30 APR 68
HAW	MAJOR DOUGLAS W. HAWKINS	JUL 68	
MUR	MAJOR BRYANT A. MURRAY	JUL 68	
MCM	LTCOL FRANCIS L. MCMULLEN	JUL 68	
MAX	MAJOR DONALD W. MAXWELL	JUL 68	
ELL	CAPT LAWRENCE J. ELLIOTT	AUG 68	
ZIM	MAJOR ROBERT C. ZIMMERMAN	SEP 68	
NEL	CAPT FRANK W. NELSON	SEP 68	
SQU	MAJOR ROBERT W. SQUIRES	SEP 68	
GRA	CAPT ROGER D. GRAHAM	OCT 68	
ZAR	CAPT LEROY D. ZARUCCHI	OCT 68	
WIL	CAPT RICHARD L. WILLEMS	OCT 68	
WIE	CAPT ERNEST J. WIEDENHOFF	NOV 68	
BRO	CAPT THOMAS E. BRONSON	DEC 68	
COH	CAPT WILLIAM A. COHEN	DEC 68	
BOW	MAJOR PETER R. BOWMAN	JAN 69	
LAN	MAJOR WALTER M. LANGFORD	MAR 69	
GIE	MAJOR LORAN W. GIERHART	MAR 69	
HEN	CAPT MICHAEL D. HENRY	APR 69	
LAW	CAPT CHARLES P. LAWS	APR 69	
MEE	CAPT JERRY L. MEEK	APR 69	
COU	CAPT LAWRENCE J. COUNTS	JUN 69	
RIC	MAJOR JAMES E. RICHEAL	SEP 69	
WAT	MAJOR MARION R. WATSON	SEP 69	
WOL	CAPT NORMAN D. WOLF	SEP 69	
ARB	LT FERDE P. ARBEIT	SEP 69	
FIS	LT ARTHUR R. FISHER	SEP 69	
TER	LT JOHN R. TERRY	SEP 69	
AND	MAJOR HOWARD V. ANDRE JR.	NOV 69	KIA 4 JUL 69
ULL	CAPT LARRY L. ULLREY	NOV 69	
CAL	MAJOR JOHN V. CALLAHAN	NOV 69	KIA 12 MAR 69
SMI	CAPT PATRICK J. SMITH	NOV 69	
MIL	MAJOR EARL E. MILAM	NOV 69	
MIC	MAJOR MICHAEL W. MICHELSEN	DEC 69	
SID	MAJOR SIDNEY I. RICHARD	DEC 69	
POT	CAPT LEON J. POTEET	DEC 69	
DAV	CAPT ROBERT C. DAVIS	DEC 69	MIA 21 MAR 69
DAL	MAJOR DAVIED R. DALTON	APR 69	
CUT	LT RICHARD R. CUTLER	APR 69	
NOL	CAPT NOLAN W. SCHMIDT	MAR 70	
FOE	MAJOR ADOLPH W. FOEH	MAR 70	
TAL	LT DAVID P. TALBERT	MAR 70	
ABR	MAJOR FLOYD J. ABRAMES	MAR 70	
WIL	LTCOL JAMES R. WILSON	APR 70	
HIC	LT EDWARD M. HICKLY	APR 70	

BER	LT THOMAS R. BERNHARDT	MAY 70
HOW	LT PAUL S. HOWE	MAY 70
POS	CAPT DELBERT A. POST	JUN 70

TDY NAVIGATOR

JAN	LT AUGUST C. JANARONE	TDY FROM 603RD ENGLAND AFB (10 JAN TO 10 MAR 69)

APPENDIX C:
NIMROD PHOTOGRAPHS

Group photo of the 609th Special Operations Squadron Nimrods, at "NKP" (Nakhon Phanom RTAFB), Thailand in 1969. Lt. Colonel Bob Stout, Squadron Commander, is standing on fuselage behind nose guns and canopy (top, center of photo). (Photo: Jim Sizemore collection)

A-26 Nimrod Aircraft on the Flight Line at Nakhon Phanom Royal Thai Air Force Base, Thailand (1966-69). (Photo from Nimrod Pilot Al Shortt's collection)

Another view of A-26 Aircraft parked on the Flight Line at Nakhon Phanom RTAFB (1966-1969). (Al Shortt collection)

Nimrod Pilot Al Shortt standing under A-26 bomb bay (1969). (Al Shortt collection)

A-26 Pilot and Gunsight in Foreground; another A-26 in Background. (Al Shortt collection)

A-26 in the Gunsight Crosshairs of Another A-26 (training flight—no ammo)(Al Shortt collection).

Major James Sizemore, A-26 pilot, at NKP (1969). (Jim Sizemore collection)

Captain Nolan Schmidt, A-26 navigator, at NKP (1969). Nolan Schmidt also served tours of duty in the Vietnam War in C-130 and F-4 aircraft.

Major Jack Mauldin, A-26 pilot, at NKP (1968-69).

Major Charles (Charlie) Vogler and TA 651 "Mighty Mouse" in SEA (1969). Major Vogler, a pilot, flew 201 combat missions with the A-26 Nimrods in 1968-69.

TA 651 "Mighty Mouse" starting No. 2 Engine at NKP (circa 1968/69).

A-26A/B-26K Counter Invader on Ramp at NKP (circa 1968/69).

TA 670 "Up Tight" on Ramp at NKP (circa 1968/69).

Great view of Pratt & Whitney R2800 Radial Engine on an A-26 at NKP (circa 1968/69). Photo shows the hard work and crucial role of the maintenance crews who kept the A-26s flying.

Reloading the .50 Caliber Nose Machine Guns on an A-26 at NKP (circa 1968-69). This photo shows the hard work and crucial role of the armament crews who kept the A-26s loaded and combat ready.

This photo captures the exhilaration of flying the A-26A Counter Invader.

This remarkable photo shows an A-26A over the open ocean being ferried from the U.S. to Thailand (or from Thailand to the U.S.). Note ferry fuel tanks just outside each engine.

Another remarkable photo of an A-26A dumping fuel from the external wing-tip tanks. This was a common practice of Nimrod crews before attacking a target to avoid AAA strikes to fuel in tanks.

View from the navigator/co-pilot seat of the A-26 as the crew flies north from NKP to Barrel Roll. The rainy season view shows a muddy Mekong River and flooded fields in Laos on far side of river.

Sunset over the Mekong River during Rainy Season; Incredibly beautiful A-26 view from pilot seat.

Nimrod Crew: Capt. Seijun ("Junie") Tengan, A-26 pilot, left, and Capt. Frank Nelson, A-26 navigator/co-pilot, right. (Photo is from Frank Nelson collection)

A-26s at Dyess AFB, Texas prior to departure to aircraft "boneyard" storage facility at Davis Monthan AFB, Arizona. (circa October 1969) Aircraft #676 was flown to the National Museum of the USAF in November 1980 and restored for the museum aircraft collection at Wright-Patterson AFB, Ohio. (See photo of next aircraft: that A-26 aircraft remains a part of the USAF Museum)(Photo of A-26s at Dyess AFB is from Frank Nelson collection)

This A-26A Counter Invader (#676) is currently on display at the National Museum of the USAF at Wright Patterson AFB, Ohio. It was one the first six A-26A aircraft to arrive at Nakhon Phanom RTAFB, Thailand in 1966. (Photo is reprinted by permission of the National Museum of the USAF.)

This exciting low-level view shows an A-26 crew flying at high speed over the target during training at the Claibourne Range near England AFB, Louisiana in the summer of 1967 (photo from the Frank Nelson collection).

This A-26 crew has just plastered the target during training exercises and is pulling up and turning left after the practice bomb drop with smoke bombs at Claibourne Range in 1967 (photo from the Frank Nelson collection).

This Photo shows an A-26 crew on a landing approach during training at England AFB, Louisiana in July 1967 (photo from the Frank Nelson collection).

Photo shows legendary A-26 aircraft (#666) and crew landing at England AFB, Louisiana in July 1967. In November 1968, aircraft (#666) was assigned to the 609th Special Operations Squadron at Nakhon Phanom RTAFB, Thailand. After the war, it was put on public display at Hurlburt Field, Florida (photo from the Frank Nelson collection).

This remarkable photo shows A-26 (#666) and crew touching down during training exercises at England AFB, Louisiana in July 1967 (photo from Frank Nelson collection).

This photo shows the cockpit of A-26 aircraft (#679) in July 1967. This is the same aircraft that is the last flying A-26 in the world (photo from the Frank Nelson collection).

Photo shows Nimrod crewmembers throwing themselves into the Songkran Festival (start of the Monsoon Rainy Season in Thailand in April 1968). That's Dick Willems with pail at far left and Bob Squires at front right. Tom Owens is seated in the center of the photo. The Thai natives loved throwing water on everyone during this unique festival; the Americans loved to join in the spirit of this Thai festival (photo from the Frank Nelson collection).

Photo shows Bruce Wolfe (Captain, USAF, pilot) having a great time throwing water on an unidentified person at NKP during the Songkran Festival in April 1968 (photo from the Frank Nelson collection).

Celebration photo shows an A-26 Nimrod crewmember who has served his country and completed his combat tour in the Vietnam War (circa 1968) (photo from the Frank Nelson collection).

Captain Frank Nelson with A-26 aircraft #651 sporting new nose art (circa May 1968).

Photo shows the Clock Tower in Nakhon Phanom, Thailand (circa 1968). Incredibly, this clock tower was built by the Vietnamese in 1960. During the 1950's, Ho Chi Minh would often visit near Nakhon Phanom, where he reportedly had many supporters (photo from the Frank Nelson collection).

This photo shows the streetside vendors in the town of Nakhon Phanom, Thailand in 1968 (photo from the Frank Nelson collection).

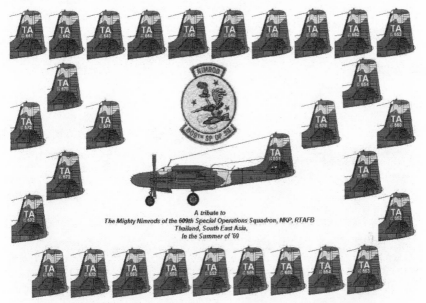

A tribute to the Mighty Nimrods in the Summer of 1969 showing 609th Special Operations Squadron Roadrunner Patch and tail numbers of A-26A Counter Invader aircraft.

Photo shows Nimrods who attended the A-26 Nimrod Reunion in 2005. Another Nimrod Reunion is scheduled for October 2007 at Hurlburt Field, Florida.

221

This beautiful painting by Harley Copic captures the essence of the Nimrods en route to yet
another combat mission in the Vietnam War. All Nimrods appreciate this beautiful painting.
This copyrighted photo of the painting is reprinted by permission of artist Harley Copic and
painting owner Paul Tobey.

APPENDIX D:
FAMILY PHOTOGRAPHS

Dianne Martin Graham and Roger Graham on their wedding day, October 26, 1963.

Dianne & Roger leaving the Chapel at Laredo AFB, Texas on their wedding day. Sword bearers were Roger's USAFA Classmates John Borling and Gary Wallace (left side) and Cliff Haney and Bob Hanneken (right side). Classmate Grant Bornzin appears at right.

Top photo shows Roger & Dianne in front of the Cadet Chapel, USAFA, while attending Class of 1963 Reunion in Colorado Springs in 2003; Bottom Photo shows Mick Roth and Roger Graham (Classmates and Nimrods).

Left photo shows Roger & Dianne in front of Roger's favorite statue at the Air Force Academy. The photo at right shows the beautiful glasswork inside the Episcopal Church (The Parish of Our Savior) near the Broadmoor Resort in Colorado Springs. Roger knew Colonel James Wright, whose father cut and placed that beautiful glassware.

Photo shows Roger's mother, Dorothy Graham Montgomery, and Roger's immediate family, on the occasion of Dorothy's 90th Birthday Celebration at Pipestem Resort, West Virginia (July 5, 2005).

Photo shows Dorothy Graham Montgomery, and her extended family, on the occasion of her 90th Birthday Celebration at Pipestem Resort, West Virginia (July 5, 2005).

Photo shows Ryan Graham in front of A-26A on display at Hurlburt Field, Florida during visit in summer of 2004 (Ryan is the son of Roger Graham and grandson of Frank Graham).

Photo of Frank Joseph Graham, husband of Dorothy Graham and father of Shirley, Daniel and Roger; member of the Greatest Generation, KIA, Battle of the Bulge, Jan. 5, 1945.

OPERATION FINAL FLIGHT

It's time to close out the story of the Nimrods (for now) who flew combat missions in the Vietnam War from 1966-69. Recently, I started reestablishing contact with Nimrods who I have not spoken with since 1967-68. Obviously, 40 years have passed since I flew with the Nimrods, and some of them have passed away. Remarkably, the Nimrods I have been able to contact still speak in the same voice, even though we have aged by four decades. Chronologically, we are much older now with gray hair replacing brown or blond hair, or no hair replacing brown or blond hair. But not surprising—we still have that same indomitable spirit. The Greatest Generation of Americans from the World War II era had that spirit. The Nimrods and their families still had that spirit during the Vietnam War. The current generation of Americans fighting in Iraq and Afghanistan, and the members of their families, still have that spirit. I sometimes worry that too many Americans outside of the military do not share or understand that magnificent American spirit of patriotism and freedom.

Having said that, I can vouch for the fact that there is a young group of Americans who fully understand and appreciate the sacrifices made by their fathers for America. The new generation is best exemplified by the founders of the A-26 Legacy Foundation, the sons and daughters of Nimrod veterans who fought for, and sometimes lost their lives while fighting for, the United States of America in the Vietnam War. I am truly humbled by this band of American sons and daughters, and one Nimrod veteran, who want to honor the Nimrods who fought (and some died) for their country in the Vietnam War. Their names are: Donald S. Vogler, Chairman, son of Lt. Colonel Charles C. Vogler, Nimrod pilot (1968-69)(now deceased); Carla Cruz Curtis, Trustee, daughter of Lt. Colonel Carlos Rafael Cruz, Nimrod pilot (KIA 29 December 1967); Michael W. Michelsen, Jr., Trustee, son of Major Michael W. Michelsen, Nimrod navigator (1968-69)(now deceased); James Sizemore, Trustee, son of Major James Elmo Sizemore, Nimrod pilot (KIA 8 July 1969); Susan Means, Trustee, daughter of Major Jack Mauldin, Nimrod pilot (1969-70); William Stetson, Webmaster, grandson of Lt. Colonel Charles C. Vogler, Nimrod pilot (1968-69) (now deceased); Major Lee D. Griffin (USAF-Ret.), CPA/Treasurer, Nimrod pilot (1968-69). They have established the A-26 Legacy Foundation (see website at www.a-26legacy.org) and have a plan to purchase the last remaining flyable A-26A for the American public. That aircraft, referred to as "Special K," has recently been flown out of Billings, Montana on fire suppression missions. The mission of the A-26 Legacy Foundation, **Operation Final Flight**, is to acquire and operate the world's "Last" airworthy Douglas A-26A/B-26K Counter Invader as a "flying museum"...dedicated to Nimrods for time immemorial... and to share their historic aircraft with air show visitors nationwide (especially younger Americans) in a tailored educational format designed to raise public awareness of those heroic veterans and their incredible airplane that flew in the service of the United States Air Force during the Vietnam War. Please visit this website, where many Nimrod A-26 photos appear in vivid color, and please make tax-deductible donations to support these young Americans as they pursue **Operation Final Flight** as a means of honoring their fathers who served their country in the Vietnam War. The following incredible photographs show the last flyable A-26A (B-26K) to come off the assembly line at On Mark Corporation, Van Nuys, California in the mid-1960s.

Special "K" at Billings, Montana (circa 2007). This aircraft (64-17679) is the worlds "Last" flying A-26A/B-26K Counter Invader.

This incredible A-26A cockpit photograph shows the flight controls and instrument panel. The pilot seat is at left and the navigator/co-pilot seat is at right.

Special "K" in front of hangars at Billings, Montana.

Another view of Special "K."

Special "K" at rest outside hangar at Billings, Montana.

Special "K" at Billings, Montana; crew excited about another flight aboard the legendary A-26A.

The Nimrods loved flying and we were honored to fly for the United States of America. **Operation Final Flight** will keep Nimrod history alive for all Americans.

Roger D. Graham
Nimrods, 2007